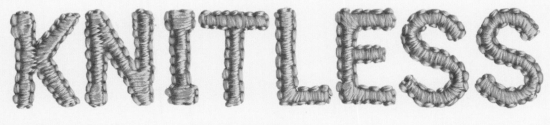

KNITLESS

50 No-Knit, Stash-Busting Yarn Projects

LAURA MCFADDEN

Running Press
PHILADELPHIA · LONDON

Copyright © 2015 by Laura McFadden
Photography © 2015 by Allan Penn
A Hollan Publishing, Inc. Concept

Published by Running Press,
A Member of the Perseus Books Group

Books published by Running Press are available at special discounts for bulk purchases in the United States by corporations, institutions, and other organizations. For more information, please contact the Special Markets Department at the Perseus Books Group, 2300 Chestnut Street, Suite 200, Philadelphia, PA 19103, or call (800) 810-4145, ext. 5000, or e-mail special.markets@perseusbooks.com.

ISBN 978-0-7624-5664-2
Library of Congress Control Number: 2015937007

E-book ISBN 978-0-7624-5803-5

9   8   7   6   5   4   3   2   1
Digit on the right indicates the number of this printing

Designed by Susan Van Horn
Edited by Kristen Green Wiewora
Typography: Didact Gothic, Berthold Akzidenz Grotesk, and True North Script

Running Press Book Publishers
2300 Chestnut Street
Philadelphia, PA 19103-4371

Visit us on the web!
www.runningpress.com

To my husband, Mathew, who keeps the trains
running no matter what.
To my son, Ray, my inspiration for living.

Table of Contents

Introduction

y love of yarn started in the 1970s when my mom's friend Diane visited us at our suburban southern New Jersey home. My eyes grew as big as saucers when I saw her crocheting a belt at our kitchen table. "How do you do that?" I asked. I was mesmerized. Diane gave me my first crochet lesson, which I immediately put into practice by stitching tube dresses for my Malibu Barbie. It never occurred to me until now that this particular Barbie, hailing from sunny California, probably didn't have much need for knitwear.

Since I never took a class or cracked a book on the subject, I was the ultimate hack crocheter. I started making up my own patterns for scarves, hats, sweaters, and more—never knowing what kind of stitch I was actually doing. Finally, when my son was born, I started reading the instructions on a variety of stitches and how to follow a pattern. I started crocheting and knitting baby sweaters for everyone who had recently had an infant. I've tried every imaginable craft, but this is the one that has stuck with me all through the years. I love the idea that you can turn a single strand of yarn into a magnificent piece of fabric.

So when I began to write *Knitless: 50 No-Knit, Stash-Busting Yarn Projects*, I got to work. What could one do with a leftover ball of yarn? Or what if you never learned how to knit or crochet? This could be the ultimate book for you. A lampshade, a chair cover, a necklace, a scarf, a picture frame, a card, what else? Let your imagination go. The projects on the following pages are just the beginning.

Laura McFadden

Chapter One

FOR THE HOME

Sputnik Lampshade Revisited

In 1957, the Soviets launched the first satellite, called Sputnik. This scientific wonder influenced industrial and textile designers, who used the space-age starburst designs on everything from wallpaper to chandeliers. Travel at the speed of light to present day with this cleaner, more modern take that will fit into your own personal space.

MATERIALS

Sputnik template (page 134)

Modern lamp with white shade

Cellophane tape

Awl

Tapestry needle

5 feet each of worsted weight yarn in five colors (light and dark turquoise, dark green, olive green, and orange)

1 Make five black and white copies of the Sputnik template.

2 Place the designs equally around the outside of the lampshade and tape into place on the top and bottom of the lampshade.

3 Using an awl, puncture the center hole and all the holes around the Sputnik template.

4 Remove the templates once you have done this all the way around the entire lampshade.

5 Single thread your first color of yarn onto the needle and tie a double knot at the end.

6 Going in from the inside of the lampshade, thread the yarn through the center hole of one of the Sputnik designs and pull the yarn through until the knot secures the yarn. The needle should now be through the front of the lampshade.

7 Embroider the starburst, always beginning with the center hole before embroidering the next ray.

8 Tie a knot at the end of the string on the inside of the shade, and cut off the remaining yarn.

9 Change your yarn color and repeat Steps 1 to 8 for each burst all the way around the lamp.

TIP: *Always consider the room for which you are making this, and choose your color palette to coordinate.*

Pom-Pom Chair

Fluffy balls gone wild! Brighten up a teenager's room, modern office, or even a nursery with a seat that's sure to make a statement. This is a great project to do with kids because pom-poms are so much fun to make, and you'll need a lot to cover the chair completely.

MATERIALS

2½- to 3½-inch pom-pom maker

8 to 10 (170-yard) skeins medium weight yarn in multiple colors

Embroidery needle

Small, sharp scissors

Metal upholstered chair

1   Follow the instructions on the pom-pom maker. Make about 140 pom-poms (depending on coverage needed for your particular chair), leaving the tails of the center knot about 8 inches long.

2   Thread the tails through the needle and sew the pom-poms onto the chair, placing them next to each other until the entire chair is covered.

TIP: *After you've sewn the pom-poms onto the chair, use a hot glue gun to make the pom-poms even more secure.*

⓷ Picture Perfect Earring Frame

Master your organization skills with this practical and attractive earring holder. It's so much easier to make sound fashion choices when you are able to see all of your options displayed in clear view.

MATERIALS

Clear craft glue

Disposable bowl

14.5 x 17-inch frame (or size of your choice) with flat front

1-inch-wide foam paintbrush

5 yards worsted weight yarn in each of six colors (teal, orange, navy, red, olive, and off-white)

Scissors

4 (12-inch) pieces 18-gauge raffia-wrapped floral wire

Heavy-duty stapler and staples

1 Pour the glue into the bowl.

2 Start on the top left side of the frame, and paint a swath of glue about 2 inches wide on the front of the frame.

3 Wrap the yarn around the frame, pressing it into the glue, and keeping the strands close together. Cut the end of the yarn on the back side of the frame once you are ready to switch colors. Add a dab of the glue to keep the yarn in place.

4 Start the second color, and repeat Steps 2 and 3. Continue brushing glue on the front of the frame as you work your way across.

5 Let it dry for one hour.

6 Stretch the four pieces of raffia wire across the inside of the frame, stapling them taut onto the back of the frame.

VARIATION: *For a different look and for holding stud earrings, a piece of window screen can be used in place of the wire. Cut it to fit your frame and staple it tightly to the back of the frame.*

④ No-Knit Yarn-Bombed Chair

Reduce your carbon footprint by darning your old sweaters onto a chair. You can also consider visiting your local thrift store for supplies. The owl sweater inspired the bird theme here, but a deer sweater could invoke pine trees, a forest-green palette, and related flora and fauna. Let your imagination be your guide.

MATERIALS

FOR THE CHAIR:

5 to 6 different sweaters in a variety of patterns and coordinating colors

Hard-backed chair with spindles

Scissors

1 (2-pound) bag of polyester stuffing for the seat

Staple gun (electric optional) and staples

10 yards each of sport weight yarn in two coordinating colors (I used yellow and pink)

Yarn needle

FOR THE EMBELLISHMENTS:

Knitted sweater (I used pink)

10 yards sport weight yarn for trim (I used grass green)

I-crochet hook (optional)

Dressmaker pins

Small eyehook

2 (3- to 4-inch) decorative birds

3-inch birdcage decoration

12 inches (16-gauge) craft wire

Pom-pom maker

For the chair:

1. Choose a sweater to cover the seat of the chair, and cut it down to cover the seat plus an additional 2 inches all the way around.

2. Place a few layers of stuffing on the seat of the chair, and trim to fit. Place the sweater over the seat, and staple the sweater edges to the underside of the chair seat, starting in the front middle and the back middle, and the middle sections of the sides of the chair seat. Work your way out to the edges. You may have to snip parts of the sweater to get it to fit around the vertical spindles or back of the chair. If this is the case, fold the ragged sides of the sweater under as you are pulling and stapling.

3. Hold a sweater sleeve up to one of the spindles in the back of your chair and cut a piece to fit around the spindle plus 1 inch extra all the way around.

4. Measure 3 arm's lengths of coordinating yarn, cut, and thread the yarn needle.

5 Wrap the piece of sweater around the spindle, then pull the edges together, hiding the rough edges underneath, and darn or stitch them together.

6 Follow Steps 3 to 5, cutting pieces of the sweaters to fit each part of the chair until all the sections of the chair are covered.

For the embellishments:

7 Make a flower by cutting the ribbed band or bottom edge off the pink sweater, about 2 inches wide.

8 Cut the band at the seam to make one long piece of knitted material.

9 Fold the sweater material in half. Then wind the fabric around itself into a coil, leaving about 8 inches as a tail.

10 Measure 1 arm's length of pink yarn, thread the needle with the single strand (not doubling it over), and tie a knot in the end. Starting in the middle of the flower, sew through the middle of all of the layers of the coil (see fig. a) beginning at 12 o'clock, then 2 o'clock, 4 o'clock, 6, 8, and 10 o'clock until you've gone completely around the coil.

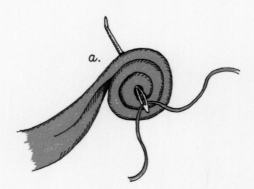

11. With the remaining 8 inches of sweater material, make it look a little more petal-like by gathering and "bunching" it up around the flower. Sew through the last layer, working counter-clockwise until you have reached the end of your fabric (see fig. b).

12. Leave an extra ½ inch at the end, tuck the cut edges under, and sew them securely in place.

13. Sew the flower onto the chair back (as shown on page 17).

14. Measure 6 yards of green yarn for a vine for your flower. Braid an 8-foot length of green cord (alternatively, crochet a single chain). Pin it onto the chair, wrapping it around the spindles, around the back of the chair, and around the legs. Single thread 4 yards of the remaining green yarn, and sew the vine onto the chair. Tie, knot, and cut the end of the yarn.

15. Use the remaining yarn on the needle to embroider some leaves onto the vine.

16. Screw the eyehook into the center of the underside of the seat, place the bird in the cage, and hang the birdcage from the eyehook. Wire the other bird onto the top right spindle.

17. Following the instructions on the pom-pom maker, make a few pom-poms to hang in a tassel. (I made one small and one medium-sized yellow, and one small pink.) Sew to the bottom of the leg of the chair so they make a cluster.

 Upcycled Lawn Chair

Give the tired plastic straps on your old lawn chair a rest, and revamp it with paracord—or parachute cord, which is a strong and lightweight nylon cord—and vivid stripes of yarn.

MATERIALS

New or recycled aluminum lawn chair frame

Heavy-duty scissors

Screwdriver, if needed

100 yards 6-mm paracord of any color (tan or light brown used here)

3 (7-ounce) skeins acrylic yarn in various colors (red, spring green, turquoise)

#13 yarn needle or weaving needle

2 ounces each of black and multicolored yarn, for detail work

1   If you are using a recycled chair, remove all webbing using scissors, and remove any screws or hardware for the webbing.

2   Place your roll of paracord on the ground inside the chair frame to start. Pull up the end of the cord and make a double knot on the front of the bottom seat frame, 3 inches in from the rounded part of the frame. Leave a 6-inch tail.

3   Pick up the cord and bring it under the center bar up toward the top of the chair and over the top of the chair back frame. Then bring the cord downward, pulling it under the center bar again, pulling it forward, and wrapping it over the bottom edge of the chair seat frame about ¼ inch from where you started.

4   Continue wrapping from the front of the chair, under the center bar, up and over the top bar of the seat back and then down under the center bar and pulling it toward the front of the seat frame next to your previous loop. **NOTE:** The cord should always wrap over the chair frame from the front and over the back of the frame.

5   When you have wrapped the chair enough times to reach about 3 inches from the other side of the seat, tie a double knot around the bottom frame edge, again leaving a 6-inch tail.

6   Unroll 3 yards of yarn, cut it, and wrap it around some cardboard. You can add on more of the same color as you run out.

7   Pull a length of yarn through the eye of the yarn or weaving needle and tie a simple knot to keep the yarn attached as you pull. Use the hook as you would a weaving needle, allowing you to go under and over multiple cords before pulling through.

8   Begin the horizontal weave with a double knot of your first colored yarn tied to the side of the frame, leaving a 6-inch tail. Tie on to the side frame of the seat about 3 inches back from the curved part of the frame.

9   Take your needle and pull your yarn under the first two rows of your cord (one top row and one bottom), and then come up from the bottom and take your yarn over the next eight rows (four top and four bottom).

10   Continue over and under eight rows at a time until you get to the point where there are only two rows of cord left (one top row and one bottom). If the pattern you wove indicates going over the last two rows, bring the yarn over the

rows and continue over the chair frame and come up from underneath to start your next row. If your weave pattern brings you under the last two rows, bring the yarn up and over the chair frame to come up from underneath to begin the next row.

> **TIP:** *No matter where your needle/yarn comes up at the end of a horizontal row, it should be wrapped over the seat chair frame and come back up from underneath. Your weaving will look tidier, and it will be easier to continue your pattern this way.*
>
> *If you run out of yarn, untie the yarn from the needle, tie on a few more yards with a square knot, and put the "new" end of the yarn through the eye of the needle and tie it there.*

11 Keep weaving until you have a stripe about 2 inches deep. You should always go over the frame and come back up from underneath, continuing to alternate the over and under weaving. When you have about a 2-inch stripe, tie off the end of the yarn to the chair frame with a double knot, leaving a 3-inch tail.

12 Starting about ½ inch from where you ended the first color, tie on the second color yarn with a double knot, and follow the directions from Step 6.

13 Repeat as above, but using your chosen accent color, make the row about 5 inches deep. Again, when finished, tie off the color, move about ½ inch back, tie on the next color, and repeat the process until the seat is covered.

> **TIP:** *You can vary the amount of room you leave between rows of color to change the amount of the vertical weave color you see. Leave a bigger gap between colors to show off more cord. For the seat of the chair, it is not recommended to leave more than an inch between the horizontal weavings, in the interest of comfort and stability.*

14 To weave the back of the chair, begin at the bottom of the chair back for ease of working. Use the same process as for the bottom of the chair. I changed my pattern for the back. Using yarn that was quadrupled, I increased the size of the stripes to about 3 inches for two stripes.

To make the design:

15 Make a basic cutout of the design. We chose a watermelon, but you could do anything. Using tape or clothespins, you can temporarily attach the cutout to find a good placement and make a basic outline of the pattern with permanent marker on the vertical cord. Remove the pattern.

16 Start with the color that will outline your pattern. For this color, you will still weave all the way from side to side, but only come over the cord where you want the color to show. Don't worry about small details; you can go back later and fill details in with a needle. When finished, tie off as in previous steps.

17 Tie on the next color, which will be the interior of your watermelon pattern. Tie the yarn directly onto the vertical cord that is closest to your outline color, and begin to weave. You will only weave from edge to edge of the inside of your watermelon rind (the green semicircle). Continue toward the innermost parts of the pattern until your design is complete.

18 When the pattern is done, weave the sections surrounding the watermelon with the turquoise yarn. Weave the yarn from one side of the chair to the other, and weave behind your watermelon, coming up on the other side of it.

19 Using the yarn needle, define the details of your design by stitching through the weaving. I added a black line to outline the watermelon and rind and made some seeds. I also added some multicolored yarn where the "bite" is missing from the watermelon. You can also fill in any spots that may look a little thin. Go back in with some red thread and add a little texture to the watermelon by sewing on lines in various directions. To finish off the design, tie a loop of red yarn around each group of turquoise yarn to bring the red color down toward the bottom of the back of the chair.

20 Using scissors, trim each tail from a knot to about 3 inches. Tuck the tails in or weave them into the design so they become invisible. Tuck in any visible knots from the cord.

TIP: *Decorative yarn—like t-shirt, ribbon, and fabric yarns—could be used in this project as well. If you want to get fancy, you can add tassels or pom-poms.*

⑥ *String Art Lampshade*

The seventies are back: what's old is new, yet again. Fire up your living space with this retro, cool lighting fixture. What works particularly well are the neutral tones of the lampshade combined with the bright orange cord. Use it over a dining or side table, or a nightstand.

MATERIALS

Drop cloth

Marker

An old kickball or other large sports ball (you'll be sacrificing it for the light fixture!)

Mod Podge

Disposable bowl

30 yards medium weight cotton yarn (off-white)

Foam paintbrush

Rubber gloves

Scissors or a sharp knife

Orange cloth lamp cord and housing for a light bulb

Light bulb, 60 watts or lower

1. Place a drop cloth on your work surface.

2. Using the marker, draw a circle on the ball, roughly 4 inches in diameter. You can use a saucer or a lid as a template to make it perfectly round. This will be where you insert the lightbulb.

3. Squeeze some Mod Podge into the bowl.

4. Run the yarn through the Mod Podge, using a foam paintbrush to coat the yarn. Then, wearing rubber gloves, wrap it around the ball, avoiding the circle you've drawn.

5. Once you've covered the ball, let it dry overnight. The Mod Podge should be completely dry and the yarn very stiff.

6. Puncture the ball with the end of your scissors or a sharp knife. Once it's deflated, pull it out of the round opening of the lampshade and throw it away.

7. Pull the cord with the plug side (as opposed to the light socket side) through the hole on the bottom of the shade, and thread it through the opposite side of the fixture. Spread some of the fibers apart on the top of the shade to get the cord through, then push them back into place once the cord has made it through the hole. Insert the light bulb through the round opening and hang the light fixture.

> **TIP:** *Use a 60-watt or lower bulb for fire safety.*

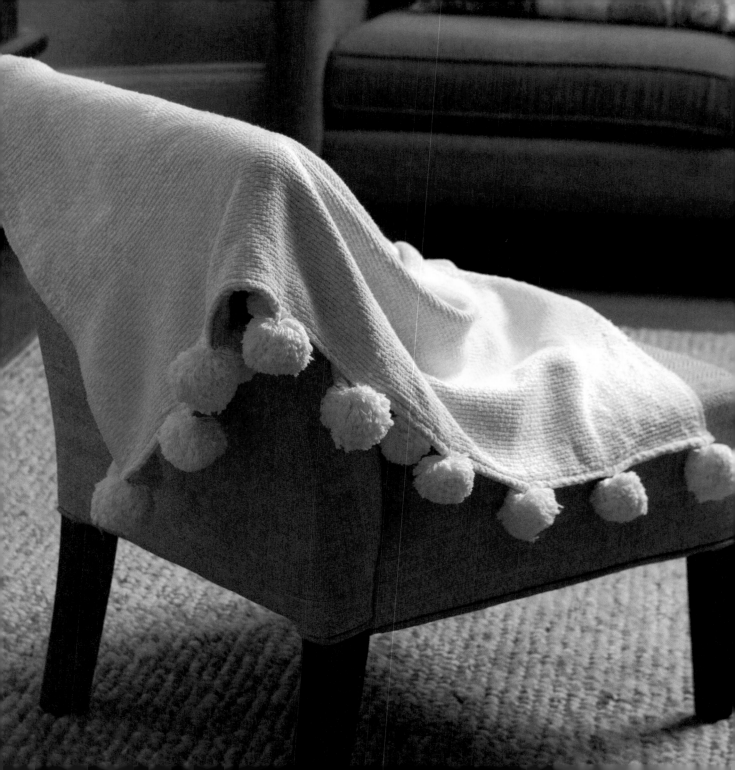

⑦ Mod Pom-Pom Throw

This forward-thinking, neon-colored blanket adds a bright, fresh look to your home décor. The giant pom-poms make it whimsical. Throw it on the back of a sofa for an extra pop of color, or wrap yourself up in it while you're reading your favorite book.

MATERIALS

Measuring tape

1 throw or blanket (plan on coordinating the yarn color for the pom-poms)

Straight pins

2½-inch pom-pom maker

8-ounce ball worsted weight cotton yarn (I used off-white)

Yarn needle

Scissors

1 Measure your throw, and decide where to place the pom-poms. I spaced my pom-poms 5½ inches apart, so I needed eighteen in total. Place straight pins to mark the spots where the pom-poms should be sewn.

2 Follow the instructions on the package of the pom-pom maker to make pom-poms with the yarn. **NOTE:** Wrap the yarn in the pom-pom maker until it is full, otherwise you will get an anemic-looking pom-pom. When you are gathering the pom-pom with the final piece of yarn, leave a tail about 6 inches long. Also, don't tie a knot into the anchoring strand until you take it off the pom-pom maker. Then pull it as tightly together as you can and knot it.

3 With a yarn needle, secure the pom-poms into place by sewing the long tails into the center of the pom-pom, then tying them to the blanket with a few knots.

4 Cut the strings down to blend with the rest of the pom-pom.

VARIATION: *For some sparkle, mix in a metallic version of your yarn. Or add a pop of color by adding in yarn that matches a secondary color in your blanket.*

⑧ Suspension Bridge Side Table

The inspiration for this project is the Zakim Bridge, which is my favorite addition to Boston's skyline. Like a suspension bridge, the empty cube under the tabletop becomes a defined space when yarn is gathered at two single points.

MATERIALS

Masking tape

Small square side table with a bottom shelf (mine was 21 inches)

Fine-tipped marker

Ruler

Drill

⅛-inch drill bit

2 small eyehooks

80 yards worsted weight yarn (mine was light green)

Scissors

Embroidery needle

80 yards worsted weight yarn (mine was turquoise)

1 Place pieces of masking tape across two opposite outside edges of the bottom shelf of the table. Using the marker, draw tick marks on the tape 1 inch apart, and ¼ inch in from the edge of the shelf. I had nineteen for my 21-inch table.

2 Repeat Step 1 on the other piece of tape.

3 Drill holes in each of the tick marks, using the ⅛-inch drill bit.

4 Place two eyehooks on the underside of the top of the table—one a few inches in from the edge on the left, and the other a few inches in on the right front side. Make sure the eyehooks do not pierce through the top of the table.

5 Measure out and cut about 10 arm's lengths of light green yarn and tie a knot at the end. Single thread the needle with the yarn. Pull the yarn up through the righthand bottom hole and pull it tightly, wrapping it around the eyehook.

6 Feed the yarn from the eyehook down through the second hole in line.

7 Continue Steps 5 to 6, feeding the yarn through the eyehook and back down through the next unfilled hole. Do this until all of the holes are filled on the front of the table. Depending on the size of your table, you may run out of yarn while you work, so just tie off the yarn on the bottom of the table and add another 10 arm's lengths to complete the side. Tie off and cut the excess yarn.

8 Switch to the turquoise yarn and repeat Steps 5 to 7 on the other side of the table.

> **TIP:** *To ensure your knot doesn't pull through the drilled holes, tie a button or a bead onto the end to make it stay in place.*

PROJECT 9 Modern Embroidered Crewel Work Pillow

Your pillow is your canvas. Your yarn is your paint. Create an eye-catching home accessory you can enjoy for years to come. The limited palette and bold design give it a minimalist, modern look that fits in well with today's contemporary décor.

MATERIALS

Template from page 135

25 x 15-inch linen pillowcase with pillow insert

Embroidery transfer paper

Straight pins

Pencil

80 yards bulky weight yarn (I chose black)

60 yards worsted weight yarn (I chose green)

Tapestry needle

Scissors

1   Photocopy the template on page 135 at 250%. Remove the pillow insert and set aside. Place the embroidery transfer paper on the front side of the pillowcase where you want the design to go. Then place the template on top of the transfer paper right-side-up, and pin them both into place with the straight pins.

2   Transfer the design onto the pillow by going over the lines of the template with the pencil. Press hard with the pencil to get the best transfer possible. Remove the template and transfer paper.

3   Single thread the yarn and embroider the design onto the pillow using the backstitch technique shown on page 149. For the smallest dots on the pillow (inside the "eye" and around the zigzag on the lefthand side), embroider French knots as shown on page 149. Refer to the photograph of the finished pillow for color breaks.

TIP: *When switching colors, remove the needle and tie off the yarn on the wrong side of the pillowcase.*

(10) Yarn and Felt CD Coasters

Reverse the curse of planned obsolescence. In other words, recycle those old CDs into coasters. This is a great way to use up your old yarn stash while saving the planet.

MATERIALS

Craft glue

Disposable bowl

4 to 6 CDs

Foam paintbrush

Two 8½ x 11-inch sheets of gray felt

Self-healing cutting mat

Utility knife and blades

Awl

4 to 6 yards each of four different shades of lightweight yarn in bright colors (blue, turquoise, orange, and yellow)

Scissors

Embroidery needle

Clear tape

1   Squeeze about a tablespoon of the glue into the bowl, and add a little water if the glue is very thick.

2   Paint the label sides of the CDs with glue, making sure you cover the entire surface. Don't place too much near the hole of the CD, or it will ooze out all over the felt.

3   Place the felt onto the self-healing cutting mat and press the CDs glue-side-down onto the felt. Let the glue set up for about 10 minutes.

4   Using the utility knife, cut the felt out around the shape of each CD.

5   Using the awl, puncture the felt in the middle of each CD, until you have a small hole for the yarn to go through.

6   Cut 3 arm's lengths of yarn, and single thread the needle with it.

7   Using the needle, pull the yarn up through the back side of the CD, leaving a 2-inch tail on the yarn. Temporarily tape the tail to the back of the CD, and pull the rest of the yarn through the felt side.

8   Wrap the yarn around the CD and up through the center hole, forming little "pie" slices with the yarn as you go around the CD. Continue working your way around the whole CD, leaving a tail several inches long on the underside of the CD.

9   Remove the tape from the starting tail, and knot the two strings together. Cut the excess yarn.

TIP: *For extra security, apply a dab of glue to the knot.*
VARIATION: *Use rainbow yarn for a self-striping effect.*

PROJECT 11 Concentric Circles Paracord Rug

As a young adult, I spent a lot of time perusing antique markets, where I fell in love with both coil and coin rugs. This contemporary hybrid of both of those rug techniques is a great way to welcome people into your home.

MATERIALS

Scissors

Invisible sewing thread

Sewing needle

120-yard skeins of bulky weight yarn in five colors (I used pale blue, seafoam green, lime green, dark gray, and dark turquoise)

150 feet (3 ⅛-inch) paracord (color complementary to palette used here)

Darning needle

Hot glue gun with glue sticks

1   Cut about 12 inches of invisible thread off the spool and double thread the sewing needle, tying the ends of the thread into a knot. Place it aside.

2   Cut 4 arm's lengths of the pale blue yarn from the skein.

3   Line up a tail of about 3 inches of yarn with the paracord (see fig. a). Wrap the yarn around the paracord and the yarn tail, covering the paracord and securing the tail (see fig. b).

4   Coil the wrapped rope into a small circle, and make a few stitches with the sewing needle and clear thread in and out of the coil to hold it all together. Tie the ends of the clear thread in a knot and cut the excess. Do not cut the paracord or the yarn.

5   Using the same yarn, single thread it with the darning needle. Continue to wrap the yarn around the paracord to cover it, and continue coiling the wrapped cord for a few inches. Then loop a stitch under and around the previous row to secure the coil (see fig. c).

a.

b.

c.

d.

6   During this process you may run out of yarn. To attach a new piece of yarn: Line up the tail of the new yarn with the remaining few inches of the old yarn parallel with the paracord. Wrap the yarn around the tail of the old yarn along with the paracord to cover both, then continue wrapping with the new yarn (see fig. d).

7   Continue coiling and sewing through the back of the previous row. Continue this process until your circle reaches 2½ inches in diameter.

8   To finish off the end of the circle, cut the end of the paracord at a diagonal, leaving about 1½ inches of unwrapped cord. Bury the tail behind the last row, and wrap the cord tightly.

9   Cut the yarn, leaving about a 3-inch tail. Weave the tail into the circle and trim.

10   Follow the chart to make 2½-, 3½-, 4½-, and 5½-inch circles in various colors.

	Pale blue	Seafoam	Lime Green	Turquoise	Gray
2½"	1	2	1	2	3
3½"		2			
4½"	3		2	2	4
5½"	1	2	3	1	1

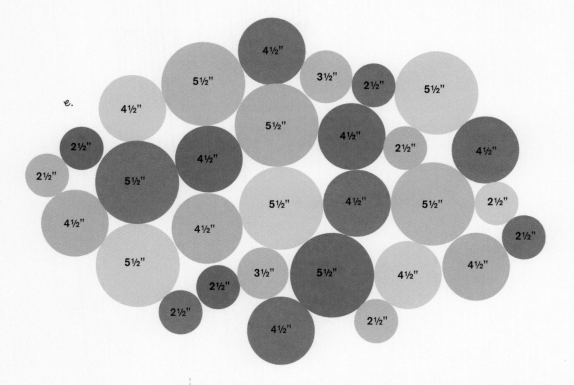

e.

11   TO ASSEMBLE THE MAT: Heat up the hot glue gun with a stick of glue in it and use it to attach all of the rug pieces together at the edges. Use fig. e and the photo for reference in assembling the different-colored circles.

12   For extra security, double thread a needle with the clear thread, flip the rug over to the wrong side, and hand sew the edges of the rug where you hot glued them.

FUN IDEA: *Using individual circles, make a set of coasters using the same technique.*

 Woven Yarn Bowl

This project incorporates traditional basket-weaving techniques in a whole new way. Using bulky weight yarn speeds up the process.

MATERIALS

145 yards bulky weight yarn (dark gray)

5 yards bulky weight yarn (magenta)

150 feet (3⅛-inch) paracord (gray or black)

Scissors

Embroidery needle

1　Follow Steps 1 to 9 of the Concentric Circles Paracord Rug on pages 35–36, making the circle 8 inches wide, and using dark gray bulky weight yarn.

2　Once your circle is 8 inches wide, you are ready to make the sides of the bowl. This is achieved by stacking the next row of paracord on top of the row you just finished instead of sewing them together side by side. This will create sides that slope upward.

3　Continue wrapping the yarn and stacking the coils until your bowl is about 3 inches high.

4　Switch to the magenta yarn. Continue working the coil until you are a little less than halfway around the bowl. Wrap about 2 inches more with the magenta yarn, but do not attach it to the row below—this will start the handle. Bend the paracord to form an arc and then attach the end of it to the row below. Continue on until you are about 2 inches from the start of your magenta cord. Make the second handle in the same manner as the first.

5　Wrap the end of the yarn tightly five times around the end of your paracord and weave the end of the yarn into the magenta portion of the bowl. Cut the end of the paracord, then sew it tightly to the row underneath it. Cut the end of the magenta yarn.

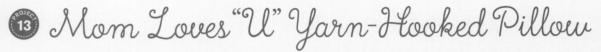

Mom Loves "U" Yarn-Hooked Pillow

This free-form make-as-you-go rug hook project is the perfect gift to give your child as they head out to camp or college, or just to reinforce to your child how much they mean to you.

MATERIALS

1 yard rug hooking linen

Yard stick

Black marker

1 (12-inch) heavy-duty quilting hoop or 12½ x 14½-inch rug hooking frame with industrial Velcro on it

Rug hook

Scissors

Leftover 12-inch scraps of worsted weight yarn in a variety of colors

Ironing board

Straight pins

1 yard faux fur (for the back of the pillow)

Sewing machine

1 pound bag polyester stuffing

Sewing needle

Coordinating thread

1. On the linen, use the marker to draw a rectangle the size that you'd like the finished pillow to be, leaving at least 6 inches all the way around. Sketch a picture or design onto the linen.

2. Place the linen in a heavy-duty quilting hoop or rug hooking frame.

3. Hold your hook in your dominant hand, and hold the yarn in the other. Place your hook through one of the linen holes and bring up a piece of your yarn, pulling it through the linen. Continue to bring up loops of yarn, which will create "stitches" in your design. Yarn loops should be as high as the yarn is thick. As you pull your hook up through the fabric, pull away from the hand holding the yarn; the yarn should be barely taut. This way, the hook won't pull out the loop you just made. All of your yarn ends should end up on top.

4. Work your way around the outline of the pillow, then fill in the outlines.

5. Cut the fabric down so it has a border of 2 inches all the way around the edges.

6. Place the finished hooked piece onto an ironing board, pin it to the board, and block it by dampening it with a wet towel. Let it dry and remove the pins.

7. Place the rug-hooked piece face-up on the work surface. Starting at the bottom of the pillow, pin the piping (flat edge facing out) around the edges, overlapping the two cut ends of the piping by about ½ an inch. Trim the cord on one end to fit inside the casing of the other end, hiding the two cut ends. Fold the excess material over the cords and pin. Machine-sew the piping onto the front of the pillow.

8. Cut the faux fur out to be the same size as the front. Place the right sides together and machine sew around all of the edges, leaving a 3-inch opening unsewn. Turn the pillow right side out. Stuff it with pillow batting and hand sew the remaining 3 inches, closing up the opening.

(14) Braided Yarn Rug

A new twist on an old classic. Your toes will be in heaven once they set foot on this super-soft carpet. Autumn hues mixed with neutral tones bring out the honey tones of a hardwood floor.

MATERIALS

13 (123-yard) skeins bulky weight yarn in various colors (six skeins of dark gray plus one for sewing the rug together, two off-white, one light gray, one burnt orange, one purple, and one gold)

Scissors

Rubber bands

Yarn needle

1 Divide a whole skein of yarn into 38-inch-long pieces. This can be done by placing two ladder-back chairs 38 inches apart, then winding the yarn between them. Once you've wound the whole skein, cut the loops at both ends.

2 Place two of the strands of yarn aside, so you can tie the ends later.

3 Gather the remaining pieces of yarn together in a bundle, and wrap a rubber band about 4½ inches in from the end. Braid the bundle of yarn until you are about 4½ inches from the other end, then tie it off with another rubber band.

4 Repeat Steps 1 to 3 with the other colors until you have twelve braids in total.

5 Remove the rubber bands, and tie the ends of the braids with the coordinating yarn you put aside earlier.

6 Using the remaining skein of dark gray yarn, single thread the yarn needle with about 4 arm's lengths of yarn.

7 Lay the braids on a flat surface to decide the order of the colors. Place two braids together side by side and hand sew the seams together. Sew all of the braids together, being sure to check the alignment as you go.

8 Cut the fringe down to about 4 inches, or to your liking.

TIP: *Before sewing the braids together, make sure to line up the braided parts, not the ends of the fringe. The fringe can always be trimmed later to even things up.*

(15) Yarn-Wrapped Vases

This group of similar but different-shaped vases creates a casual centerpiece. By starting with a beautifully colored vase and wrapping only a portion of it, you can create the perfect synthesis of color and texture. Brighten up a room by filling them with freshly picked or dried flowers.

MATERIALS

Craft glue

Disposable bowl

Newspaper

Foam paintbrush

3 vases of varying sizes

10 yards of lightweight yarn in three colors (sage green, gray blue, and orange)

Wooden skewer

Scissors

20 yards of worsted weight cotton yarn (off-white)

9 (½-inch) wooden disks or buttons (optional)

1 Pour some glue into the disposable bowl and line your work surface with newspaper. Use the foam paintbrush to paint on a wide patch of glue around the vase, two-thirds of the way down (or wherever looks best on your particular vase), and attach your colored yarn. You can leave the yarn on the ball to make wrapping easier and cut it when you have finished your band. Wrap and glue, lining the strands up so that there are no gaps, until you have about a 1-inch band of color. The wooden skewer can be used to push the strands closer together. You can hide the tail of the yarn by pushing it down into the top rows that you've wrapped. This will help with fraying. Cut the end of the yarn.

2 Continue below the band of color with another color. (I switched to off-white yarn.) Start by wrapping the new yarn over the tail of the previous color to secure it, and continue wrapping and gluing until the bottom of the vase is covered. Trim the yarn and bury the tail in the last few rows.

3 Cover one side of the wooden disk with glue. Starting in the middle of the disk, coil a piece of colored yarn on the front of the disk until the disk is covered. Make three.

4 Glue the disks to the front of the vase about ¾ inch apart.

5 Repeat steps 1 to 4 with the remaining two vases.

Spirographic Clock

Inspired by the drawing toy of the sixties, Spirograph, and another popular craft, string art, this clock takes us back in time—while helping us stay on schedule.

MATERIALS

#00 sandpaper

Sanding block

12 x ¼-inch wooden clock round with center hole

Matte gray spray paint and primer in one

Clock template from page 136

Clear tape

4 (¾-inch) silver washers

Hammer

48 (#3 ⅜-inch) blue steel-cut upholstery tacks

Utility knife

8 yards lightweight cotton yarn in each of three colors (red, orange, and yellow)

Scissors

White glue

Silver paint marker

Clock works for dial up to ⅝ inch thick

AA battery

1　Sand the face and sides of the wooden clock until they are smooth.

2　Spray paint the face of the clock, following the instructions on the can. You may want two coats for best coverage.

3　Photocopy the clock template from page 136 at 145%, cut it out, and line up the center hole of the template with the center hole of the clock round.

4　Tape the clock template to the face of the clock.

5　Place four washers on the face of the template at 12 o'clock, 3 o'clock, 6 o'clock, and 9 o'clock, each time hammering a tack into the center of the washer to hold it in place. Drive the tacks into the wood with the hammer about six times, or just enough so they don't poke through the back of the clock. Hammer the remaining upholstery tacks into the clock round in the spots designated with black dots on the template. Tear off the paper template and cut away any excess paper with the utility knife or tweezers.

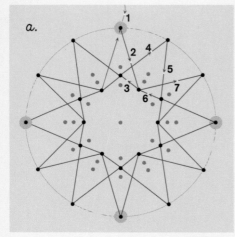

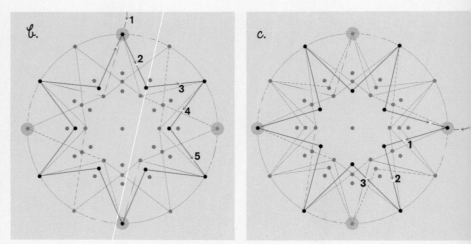

6 Measure and cut 5 arm's lengths of red yarn. Tie a knot in the yarn around the tack at 12 o'clock, leaving a tail of about 3 inches. Feed the tail underneath the washer to hide it. (Use this same technique for all of the colors of yarn in Steps 7 to 10.)

7 Wrap the yarn in a full circle around each nail, following the arrows on fig. a.

8 When you reach 12 o'clock, tie the end of the yarn to the tack, and feed the tail of the yarn under the washer to hide it.

9 Beginning with the orange yarn at 12 o'clock, wrap the yarn full circle around each nail, following the arrows (fig. b). When you come full circle back to 12 o'clock, tie the end of the yarn to the tack, and feed the tail of the yarn under the washer. Trim the excess yarn.

10 Cut another 4 yards of orange yarn and starting at 3 o'clock, wrap the yarn around the nails as shown in fig. c. Then you finish the second layer back at 3 o'clock, tie the end of the yarn to the tack, and feed the tail of the yarn under the washer. Trim the excess yarn.

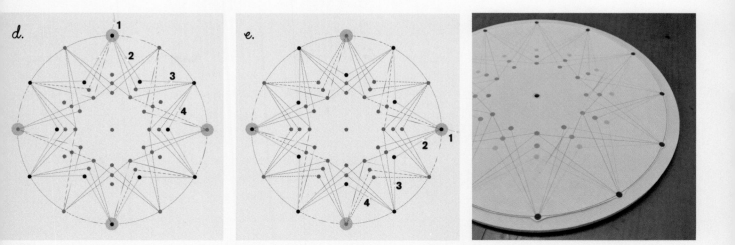

11 Beginning with the yellow yarn and starting at 12 o'clock, wrap the yarn full circle around each tack, following the arrows on fig. d, Yellow Layer 1, and fig. e, Yellow Layer 2. **NOTE:** There are two layers of yellow. When you reach 12 o'clock, tie the end of the yarn to the tack, and feed the tail of the yarn under the washer. When you finish the second layer at 3 o'clock, tie the end of the yarn to the tack and feed the tail of the yarn under the washer.

12 Using the utility knife, cut any excess yarn tails, tucking the ends under the washers. For extra security, adhere the yarn ends and washer to the clock round with a small dab of white glue, and hammer the tacks in more tightly to the clock face.

13 Use the silver paint marker to make a nice, bright rim around the outside edge of the clock.

14 Follow the manufacturer's instructions for clock assembly, and place in the center of the finished clock.

TIP: *To add a little extra sparkle to the clock, paint the tack heads with the silver marker.*

⟨17⟩ High Wire Embroidered Tissue Box Cover

Definitely not your grandmother's plastic needlepoint canvas cover. This revamp is both hip and playful, combining photographic imagery with geometric embroidery. I found this image online from a stock photography agency, and you can find a similar one to use. Or you can always cut out an image from a magazine or freehand it, if you have the drawing skills.

MATERIALS

Template from page 137

Pencil

Scissors

Clear tape

5.4 x 5.1-inch papier-mâché tissue box cover

Power drill

7/64-inch drill bit

10 yards lightweight yarn (mine was metallic orange)

10 yards lightweight yarn (mine was turquoise)

Tapestry needle

Stock art of a trapeze artist

Glue stick

1 Make two photocopies of the template from page 137. Rub the backs of the templates all over with a pencil. Cut them out and tape one to the front and one to the back of the tissue box. Firmly trace over the pattern lines on the front and back of the box with a pencil, which will transfer the pattern onto the box.

2 Drill through all of the holes marked on the templates, and then remove the paper.

3 Single thread 3 arm's lengths of orange yarn and triple knot the end. Stitch the pattern on the front of the box using the backstitch method on page 149. When you run out of yarn, cut more yarn and thread the needle.

4 Repeat Step 3 on the back of the box, using the turquoise yarn.

5 Drill two additional holes on each remaining blank side of the box at the bottom left and right corners. Single thread 2 yards of the orange yarn and embroider from the diamonds on the right front edge of the box to the lower righthand hole.

6 Turn the box to the turquoise side and single thread 2 yards of the turquoise yarn. Embroider from the lefthand diamonds down to the hole on the lower lefthand side of the box.

7 Repeat Steps 5 to 6 on the opposite, blank side of the box.

8 Print out your stock art. Cut it out and glue it onto the side of the box where the converging lines are. Here we have the high wire artist's feet centered on the top lines.

TIP: *For additional embellishments, consider covering the top of the tissue box with some orange or turquoise paper or some colorful gems.*

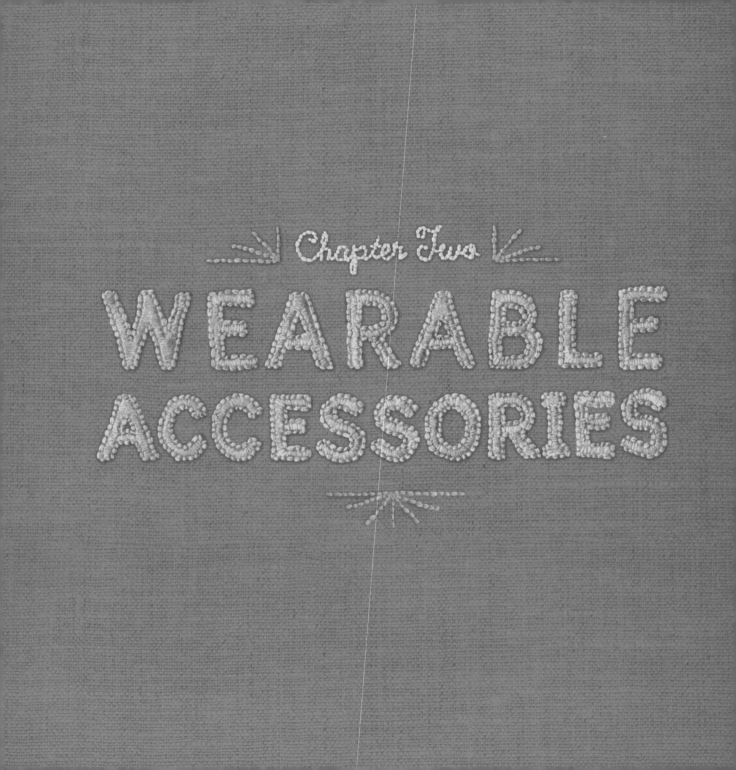

Chapter Two
WEARABLE ACCESSORIES

Wrapped Beaded Wooden Necklace

PROJECT 18

This large-bead, multicolored necklace is both casual and a statement piece of jewelry. Make this your star accessory by wearing it with a plain sweater or tee, or a simple dress.

MATERIALS

4 (10-yard) balls of lightweight yarn in various colors (tan, blue, orange, and brown)

Tapestry needle

7 (1-inch) wooden beads with large holes

Scissors

1   Double thread your needle and tie a knot at the end of it. Pull it through the center of a bead, run the needle through the center of the double threaded yarn, then pull the yarn tight. This will anchor the knot.

2   Thread the needle back through the center hole, and hide the knot in the center of the bead.

3   Loop the yarn around the bead and pull it up through the center hole again and again until the bead is completely covered in yarn. Tie a knot at the end of the yarn, and cut any excess yarn off. All together you will make two tan, two blue, two orange, and one brown bead.

4   Cut six 48-inch lengths of the brown yarn. Thread the yarn and then place the beads on the yarn in the following order: tan, blue, orange, brown, orange, blue, and tan.

5   Once you've got all six yarns threaded through the beads, center the beads on the yarn. Tie a double knot on either side of the bead ends to keep them in place.

6   Braid the yarn on either side of the beads. Each braid should measure about 8 inches when complete. Tie a knot at the end of the braid on both sides. Trim the ends of the necklace, leaving a tail on each end of 4 inches so you can make the necklace into a bow.

Totally Tubular Bracelet

Fiber meets rubber with this modern, minimalist version of the friendship bracelet. The clear rubber tubing provides the housing to feed the yarn in two opposing directions.

MATERIALS

Ruler

⅜-inch x 10-foot clear vinyl/PVC tubing (available in the plumbing section at hardware stores)

Marker

Heavy-duty garden clippers or kitchen shears

5 yards of lightweight yarn (orange)

5 yards of lightweight yarn (yellow)

Scissors

2 tapestry needles

2 (½-inch) glass beads

1   With your ruler, measure out ten 1-inch pieces of tubing, and mark them with your marker. Cut them with the garden clippers.

2   Measure, then cut, 3 arm's lengths each of the orange and yellow yarn.

3   Single thread the orange yarn with one tapestry needle and single thread the yellow yarn with the other. Tie both yarns together in a knot, leaving a 12-inch tail.

4   Feed the orange yarn into one end of the 1-inch tube, then feed the yellow yarn into the opposite end of the tube. The two yarns will cross over each other inside the tube.

5   Stack a second piece of 1-inch tubing above the first and repeat Step 4 (see fig. a). Do this until you have all 10 pieces of tube strung onto the bracelet. Knot the two ends of the bracelet together at the base of the last tube.

6   To make the bracelet adjustable: See page 79, Modern Macramé-Ringed Friendship Bracelets, figs. e-1, e-2, and f.

7   Slide the glass beads onto the tail ends and tie one or two knots at the end, leaving about 3 inches.

VARIATION: *If you don't need to make the bracelet adjustable, you can use a lobster claw or a magnetic clasp.*

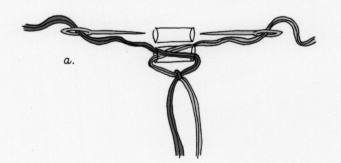

a.

PROJECT 20 Totally Tubular Belt

A longer version of the Totally Tubular Bracelet that looks great with jeans or your favorite dress.

MATERIALS

Ruler

⅜-inch x 10-foot clear vinyl/PVC tubing (available in the plumbing section at hardware stores)

Marker

Heavy-duty garden clippers or kitchen shears

15 yards of lightweight yarn (orange)

15 yards of lightweight yarn (yellow)

15 yards of lightweight yarn (green)

Scissors

2 tapestry needles

1 With your ruler, measure out fifty-five 1-inch lengths of tubing, and mark them with your marker. Then cut them with the garden clippers.

2 Measure, then cut, 8 arm's lengths each of the orange, yellow, and green yarn. Put them aside and then measure and cut 8 arm's lengths more of each color.

3 Single thread the orange, yellow, and green yarn onto one tapestry needle. Then single thread the other needle with the other three strands of orange, yellow, and green yarn. Tie the ends of all six strands together in a knot, leaving a 20-inch tail.

4 Feed one needle into one end of a 1-inch piece of tube, then feed the second needle into the opposite end of the tube. The two sets of yarn will cross over each other inside the tube.

5 Take another piece of 1-inch tubing and repeat Step 4 (see fig. a on page 57). Repeat this until you have all 55 tubes strung onto the belt. Knot the two bundles of yarn together at the base of the last tube.

6 Braid one end of the belt about 7 inches, then tie the ends in a knot, leaving a 2-inch tail. Repeat this on the other end of the belt.

TIP: *Even though this belt is adjustable, these instructions can be altered to fit a narrower or wider waistline. You can use fewer or more pieces of plastic tubing to fit.*

(21) From Here to Infinity Braided Scarf with Pom-Poms

A fresh take on the infinitely popular infinity scarf. The more you loop it around, the warmer you'll feel on those cold winter days.

MATERIALS

Scissors

2 (106-yard) skeins off-white bulky weight yarn

Measuring tape

⅜-inch pom-pom maker

8 yards sport weight yarn in three colors (teal, green, and orange)

1 Cut your off-white yarn into 15-foot pieces, then divide the pieces into three sections. Braid each skein of off-white yarn, then join the two braids in a knot.

2 Follow the instructions on the pom-pom maker to create two teal pom-poms, two orange pom-poms, and two green pom-poms. Leave long tails on each pom-pom. You will use these tails to attach the pom-poms to the scarf.

3 Pull the tails of the pom-poms through the off-white braided scarf, randomly placing them around the braid until you like the placement, and knot them onto the braid.

TIP: *Try tying the yarn to the back of a chair before you braid it. This will give you more control, ensuring a more even-looking braid.*

Pom-Pom Covered Slippers

PROJECT 22

Have you ever seen the old Hollywood movies where the stars come out in their luxurious sleepwear? These look nothing like those slippers of the stars. But you can still make a grand entrance from your boudoir with these show-stopping beauties.

MATERIALS

About 80 (½-inch) pink and 15 orange pom-poms (made with leftover stash and ½-inch pom-pom maker)

Sewing thread (pink)

Yarn needle

Pair of plush slippers (pink)

1   Follow the instructions on the package of the pom-pom maker to make pom-poms with the yarn. **NOTE:** Wrap the yarn in the pom-pom maker until it is full; otherwise you will get an anemic-looking pom-pom. When you are gathering the pom-pom with the final piece of yarn, leave a tail of about 6 inches. Also, don't tie a knot into the anchoring strand until you take it off the pom-pom maker. Then pull it as tightly together as you can and knot it.

2   Double thread the needle with a 6-inch pom-pom tail.

3   Thread the tail of the pom-pom from the outside to the inside of the slipper, then bring the yarn back to the outside of the slipper and tie it in a tight knot. Cut the tail to the same length as the pom-pom fringe. Repeat to attach all pom-poms to the slippers.

4   Cover the slippers with pink pom-poms, interspersing the occasional orange one here and there.

5   Repeat Steps 2 to 4 on the second slipper.

VARIATION: *For a simple, subtler look, alternate pink and orange pom-poms along the top edge only of the slippers.*

Grande Dame Shoe Clips

This is a simple way to embellish your high heels or flats. The removable clips allow you to dress the shoes up or down depending on the occasion.

MATERIALS

Disposable coffee pod or a shot glass for tracing (try it out on the toe of your shoe to make sure it's not too large or small)

4 x 6-inch piece cardboard

Pencil

Scissors

Ruler

Awl

10 yards of sport weight metallic yarn (copper)

Tapestry needle

Hot glue gun with glue sticks

Rhinestone embellishments

Matching sewing thread

Shoe clip hardware

Pair of flats or heels

1 | Trace the shape of the coffee pod or shot glass onto a piece of cardboard with the pencil for the base of the clip. Make two, then cut them both out.

2 | Once you've cut them out, make tiny snips all the way around the cardboard. This will keep the yarn from slipping around too much.

3 | Measure the exact center of your cardboard circles, then poke a hole in the center of the cardboard with the awl, large enough for the yarn to go in and out many times.

4 | Pull about 6 arm's lengths of the yarn off the skein, and cut with scissors. Double thread the yarn on the tapestry needle and tie a knot at the end.

5 | Pull the threaded needle up through the center of one of the cardboard circles, running the yarn around the outside of the circle and back up through the hole. Repeat until the entire surface of the cardboard is covered.

6 | Tie a knot in the back of the shoe embellishment and trim with scissors. Repeat Steps 5 to 6 on the second cardboard circle.

7 | Heat up the hot glue gun with a stick of glue in it, and hot glue a rhinestone to the center of each shoe embellishment.

8 | When the glue is dry, double thread the tapestry needle with the sewing thread and tie a knot at the end.

9 | Sew the shoe clip hardware onto the back of the shoe embellishment and clip onto shoes.

VARIATION: *For an everyday set, use multicolored yarn and no rhinestone embellishment, or replace the rhinestone with a cute button.*

No-Knit One-Hour Scarf

Simple. Easy. Warm. 'Nuff said.

MATERIALS

Scissors

123 yards super bulky weight yarn (teal)

Sewing machine

Sewing thread (gray)

1 Cut the bulky weight yarn into 63-inch pieces. Use up all of the yarn.

2 Align the pieces side by side on your work surface. Feed the whole bundle underneath the presser foot of your sewing machine, placing the needle about 7 inches in from the cut ends on one side.

3 Sew perpendicularly across the yarn, holding on to the yarn bundle tightly as you run it through the sewing machine.

4 Sew back and forth from edge to edge about six times, not worrying about the stitches being even. The uneven nature of the sewing will make it feel even more handmade.

5 Repeat Step 4 every 6 inches, sewing across the yarn bundle to secure the strands of yarn. Do this nine times total.

6 Trim the edges of the yarn evenly.

VARIATION: *An even simpler "no-sew" version can be made by using 3 different colors of yarn. Measure and cut out six 100-foot strands of each color. Take the three different colors of yarn and twist them into a spiral. Gather the ends with a piece of yarn, leaving an excess tail of 14 inches. Tie the pieces together tightly. Trim the tail ends at various lengths to get a cascading effect.*

The Makeover Sneaker

Upgrade ordinary canvas shoes from blah to beautiful using this free-form embroidery design.

MATERIALS

Scissors

10 yards each of lightweight yarn in four colors (red, magenta, orange, and yellow)

Embroidery needle

Canvas shoes

2 feet (34-gauge) brass wire

1   Cut 3 arm's lengths of all the colors of yarn.

2   Thread the needle with the red yarn. Using a backstitch with small stitches (see page 149), make a zigzag stitch across the top panel of the shoe (use the photo for reference). It will look like a chevron pattern when completed. Tie a knot in the underside of the sneaker, and cut the thread close to the knot.

3   Thread the needle with the magenta yarn and embroider an outline around the red yarn top and bottom using a backstitch. Tie a knot in the underside of the sneaker and cut the thread close to the knot. Thread the needle with the orange yarn, and embroider with a backstitch around the pattern, top and bottom.

4   Thread the needle with the yellow yarn and follow Step 3, this time outlining the orange yarn. Do not knot or cut the yarn.

5   Continue stitching with the yellow around the pattern, filling in the space between the zigzags. Use the photo for reference. Tie a knot on the underside of the sneaker, and cut the yellow yarn close to the knot.

6   OPTIONAL TASSELS (make 2): Cut one 6-inch piece of every color of yarn for each tassel, and two 12-inch pieces of magenta yarn, one for each tassel. Set aside the yarn for the second tassel.

7   Lay your 12-inch piece of magenta yarn horizontally across your workspace and place the 6-inch pieces in a bundle on top of the magenta yarn in the center.

8   Gather up the yarn bundle and tie the magenta yarn in a tight knot.

9   Cut a 12-inch length of the wire and wrap it around the tassel, about ¼ inch down from the top of the tassel.

10 Cut the ends of the tassel to about 1 inch.

11 Thread the magenta yarn onto the needle and sew the tassel to the bottom "V" on the shoes. Knot the yarn on the inside and trim the ends.

12 Repeat Steps 7 to 11 on the other sneaker.

VARIATION: *Make a braid out of some leftover yarn, and hot glue it around the perimeter of the sneaker.*

㉖ Button Cocktail Ring

This piece of jewelry, with all of its boldness, demands to be noticed on your finger—but don't confine it to evening galas. The yarn makes it more casual and fun for everyday wear.

MATERIALS

Fabric glue

1-inch dome-shaped wooden button

2 yards each of tatting yarn or embroidery floss in four colors (pink, purple, light blue, and off-white)

Toothpick

Scissors

Pencil

4-inch piece of velvet or ultra suede in coordinating color

Hot glue gun with glue sticks

Adjustable ring

1 Place a small amount of fabric glue into the middle of the button cover.

2 Tightly coil a small piece of pink yarn in the center of the button. Use a toothpick to help guide the thread. Cut the end.

3 Coil a small amount of purple yarn around the pink for about 2 rows, changing the shape from round to square. Continue adding small amounts of glue to the button as you go along.

4 Coil a small amount of off-white yarn around the purple for one row.

5 Complete the square with two rows of light blue.

6 Create four separate "rainbows" around the edge of the square. Each pair of rainbows opposite one another will be identical. Make sure to leave at least an extra ¼ inch of yarn to tuck to the underside of the ring at the end of each row. Glue all the ends to the underside of the button.

OPPOSITE RAINBOWS A:
One row off-white
Two rows purple
Two rows pink
One row off-white
Two rows light blue
One row off-white
Three rows pink

OPPOSITE RAINBOWS B:
One row off-white
Two rows light blue
Two rows pink
One row off-white
Two rows purple
One row off-white
Two rows light blue
One row pink

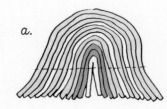 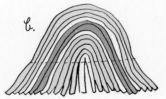

a.   b.

7 Trace the shape of the button on the back side of the velvet and then cut it out. The velvet should be just a tad smaller than the button, so it doesn't show from the top. Glue it to the back of the button.

8 Heat up the hot glue gun with a stick of glue in it, and adhere the adjustable ring to the back of the velvet.

TIP: *For a little extra bling, sew a seed bead or rhinestone to the center of the button.*

㉗ Woven Cutout Belt

I always meant to make a spring scarf, yet the yarn languished for years, gathering dust in my closet. Also in my closet was a laser-cut leather belt that just needed a little something special. Here that beautiful yarn makes its debut woven into a much hipper-looking belt. You could also use a leather belt that is woven, or that has any kind of cutout design in the strap.

MATERIALS

142 yards variegated ribbon yarn

Scissors

Yarn needle

Gridded belt

Fabric glue

1   Measure out 4 arm's lengths of the ribbon yarn and cut it.

2   Single thread the ribbon yarn on the needle.

3   Start on the inside (non-showing side) at the bottom edge at one end of the belt. Weave the yarn through every other hole, leaving a tail of about 2 inches on either end. Cut the yarn.

4   Follow Steps 1 to 3 for the top edge. For this project, I wove only the outside edges, leaving the inside grid unwoven to accommodate for adjusting the belt buckle.

5   Tie the ends together in a knot, and hide the knot on the underside of the belt. Trim the excess yarn. For extra security, glue the knot with a very small dab of the fabric glue.

VARIATION: *Cutout patterns are all the rage. Try this same technique woven into pocketbooks, bracelets, or shoes.*

Boho Wrapped Paracord Necklace

"Boho" or "Bohemian" style is all about the layering of accessories. This all-in-one multilayer necklace has that carefree, gypsy feel.

MATERIALS

Hot glue gun with glue sticks

1 yard paracord (tan)

1 paracord closure

5 yards each of lightweight cotton yarn in four colors (pink, light purple, brown, and tan)

5 yards lightweight acrylic yarn (metallic red-orange)

Scissors

Embroidery needle

White craft glue

Variety pack of assorted wooden beads

70 (3 mm) orange wooden beads

3-inch-wide piece cardboard

1 (20 mm) unfinished wooden bead

1. Heat up the hot glue gun with a stick of glue in it, and place a dab of glue on one end of the paracord.

2. Place the end of the paracord into the socket of the closure and hold it in place for a minute until the glue sets up. Repeat to glue the other piece of the closure on the other end of the paracord.

3. Take the tan yarn and hold a tail of about 3 inches of yarn parallel with the paracord, tail facing in. Start wrapping it around the paracord for about 3 inches to secure the tail.

4. Follow Step 3 for all the remaining colors, changing the color of yarn randomly to suit. To attach a new piece of yarn: Cut the old yarn to leave a tail of a few inches. Hold it and the tail of the new yarn against the paracord. Wrap the new yarn around the tails to cover both. The idea is for the colors to have an uneven, random feeling.

5. When you finish wrapping the yarn all the way around the paracord, thread the embroidery needle with the last piece of yarn and sew it through the layer of paracord. Tie a knot in the end of the yarn. Cut the tail and add a small dab of white glue to secure the knot.

6. For the beaded strands in the middle: single thread the embroidery needle with a piece of tan yarn about 18 inches long. Tie a knot in the end, leaving a 6-inch tail. String on a variety of the wooden beads until they measure 6½ inches.

7. Fold the wrapped paracord part of the necklace in half and measure about 4½ inches from the center on both sides. Sew the beads onto the paracord to make a second tier in the necklace, as shown in the photo. Do this on both sides.

8   Using a piece of tan yarn, tie a knot leaving a 6-inch tail. Single thread the yarn and string on 70 of the orange wooden beads (or until the length of strung beads measures 12¼ inches).

9   Sew the beads onto the paracord, about 10½ inches up from the center of the paracord. Do this on both sides. Knot the ends and cut any excess yarn off.

10 FOR THE TASSEL: Wrap the tan yarn around the cardboard about 30 times. Pull the yarn off the cardboard, keeping the shape intact. Cut a 6-inch strand of tan yarn and wrap it around the top of the loops of yarn you just made, tying them in a tight bundle. Tie a knot in the strand of yarn but don't cut the ends.

11 Slide the 20 mm wooden bead onto the tassel and white glue it in place.

12 Cut the ends of yarn at the bottom of the tassel so they measure about 2 inches from the bottom of the wooden bead.

13 Thread the uncut ends of yarn at the top of the tassel onto the embroidery needle. Wrap the strands around the center of the paracord several times and tie them in a knot. Feed the remaining strands in through the center of the bead to hide them.

TIP: *When you are finishing off the ends of your beading, hide them by burying the remaining yarn strands back through the first few beads. Then cut the ends of the yarn. Add a little dab of glue for extra hold.*

PROJECT 29 Modern Macramé-Ringed Friendship Bracelets

These brightly colored metallic bands, with the addition of shiny rings, are the modern, more stylish version of the ones worn by young people as a token of friendship.

MATERIALS

Scissors

Measuring tape

5 yards of fingering weight metallic yarn (blue, purple, and magenta shown)

Gold-colored connector circles (one for each bracelet)

Nail driven into a board, to hold your bracelet while you work

Tapestry needle

2 small gold beads for each bracelet

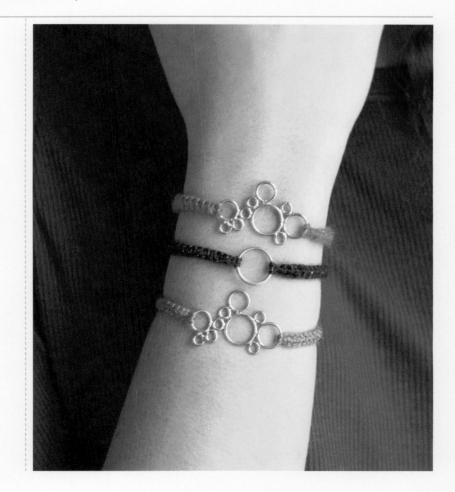

1   Cut five 30-inch-long pieces of yarn and place three to the side. Take one piece of yarn, fold it in half, and slip-knot it through one of the end circles on the connector circle. Place your connector circle on the nail on the board (fig. a).

2   Take another piece of the 30-inch yarn and slip it under the 2 hanging pieces of yarn. It should be perpendicular to the one on the board.

3   Make a figure eight with the yarn, and fold the tails into each of the loops as shown in fig. b. Pull the ends tight.

4   To start the macramé, take the piece of yarn farthest to the right and make a "P" shape with it. Take the left-most piece of yarn, overlap the tail of the righthand yarn, and bring it under both the middle strands and through the back of the "P"-shaped loop. Then pull it tight (see fig. c).

5   Repeat Step 4 with the lefthand strand, this time making a backwards "P" when you start (see fig. d). This can sometimes get a little confusing. A good rule of thumb is to make the "P" on whichever side you see the bump of the knot from the previous row.

6   Keep switching from right to left until the bracelet measures half the circumference of your wrist.

a.

b.

c.

d.

7 Leave the excess yarn hanging and begin the other side of the connector circle. Repeat Steps 1 to 7 until both sides of the bracelet are the same length.

8 Single thread the yarn and weave the two ends of the bracelet back into the macramé.

9 Do the same on the other side.

10 To make the bracelet adjustable, turn the bracelet to the back side and form a loop with the remaining strands (see fig. e-1). Wrap the remaining strand of yarn so it's perpendicular to the four strands of yarn on the back of the bracelet (see fig. e-2). This is done in a similar manner to Steps 2 and 3.

11 Macramé about seven rows. Weave in the ends, making sure you don't catch the other four strands of yarn in the center. If you do, it will prevent the bracelet from being adjustable (see fig. f).

12 Pull the ends so the bracelet is tight. Slide the small beads onto the tail ends and tie one or two knots at the end, leaving about 3 inches.

13 Repeat Step 12 on the ends on the other side.

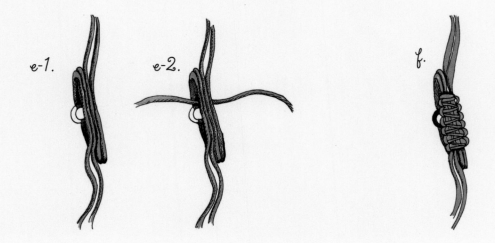

e-1.   e-2.   f.

Sophisticated Tribal Tassel Necklace

This elegant necklace takes its cues from both Africa and Europe, with its African tassels and its rhinestone sparkles. Wake up a plain t-shirt or your favorite LBD with this dazzling collar.

MATERIALS

18-inch-long chunky chain (with a gauge large enough to put three pieces of yarn through each link)

18-inch-long chains (one rhinestone chain and two other lighter-gauge chains)

Beading glue

Rhinestone chain connector crimp

Needle-nose pliers

Scissors

12 (¼-inch) jump rings

Lobster clasp

8 yards satin yarn or silk cord

Credit card

34-gauge brass wire

1   Lay your chains out in the order you would like them to be in the finished necklace. The chunky chain should go on the bottom since you are adhering the tassels to it.

2   Apply a small amount of glue to the center of your chain connector crimp. Attach the rhinestone chain on either end of the crimp and push the prongs down with your needle-nose pliers. If there are stray ends of string on either end of the rhinestone chain, tie them in a knot and cut the ends close to the knot. Apply a small dot of glue to the knot.

3   Using your needle-nose pliers, attach all of the chains together on either end, using the jump rings. Close up the jump ring on one side but leave the jump ring on the other side open. Place your lobster clasp on the open jump ring, then close up that ring.

4   Wrap the yarn around the long side of a credit card, about 40 times, then cut the yarn in half with scissors.

5   Take three strands of yarn and thread the strands through the center link of the chunky chain, until you reach the midpoint of the length of yarn. Fold the yarn in half.

6   Cut a 10-inch length of wire and wrap it tightly around the yarn, gathering it just below where the folded yarn has gone through the chain. Wrap the wire about 20 times to create the tassel.

7   Repeat Steps 5 to 6 until you have 12 tassels. Each additional tassel will be made in every other chain link, starting with the center tassel.

TIP: *Consignment shops are often a goldmine for various jewelry parts.*

 Crewel Work Beach Bag

Schlepp your stuff to sand and sea in this whimsical summer bag.

MATERIALS

**Yarn flower loom with
3 different-size looms plus
a plastic needle**

**4 yards each of sport weight
yarn in six colors (purple, pink,
orange, dark green, yellow,
and black)**

Hot glue gun with glue sticks

Template on page 139

Tape

Dark-colored transfer paper

Straight pins

**Burlap beach bag (lime
green used here)**

Number 2 pencil

1 yard dark green ric-rac

Embroidery needle

Scissors

**6-inch piece of dark
green felt**

1   Make the three different-size flowers (small, medium, and large) following the instructions included with the loom. Here I made the smallest flower pink, the medium flower orange, and the large flower purple.

2   While you are working on the flowers, heat up the hot glue gun with a stick of glue in it.

3   Photocopy two copies of the template on page 139. Tape the transfer paper to the back of the template. Position and pin one template onto the bag so the wavy line is about 3 inches up from the bottom. Transfer the design onto the bag using the number 2 pencil, following the instructions on the transfer paper package. Then remove the template and transfer paper from the bag.

4   Starting at the seam on the side of the bag, pin the ric-rac all the way around the bag. Glue the ric-rac onto the bag with the hot glue gun and remove the pins.

5   Glue the yarn flowers onto the bag in the spots shown on the transferred template.

6   Single thread the embroidery needle with some green yarn, then embroider the stems for each flower. I used a backstitch (shown on page 149).

7   Using the second copy of the template, cut out six felt leaves for the flowers. Glue the leaves to the stems as shown in the photograph of the finished bag.

8   Embroider the bee in yellow and black. Make two loops with the black yarn for the wings. Embroider the pathway of the bee in yellow.

VARIATION: *A hula girl and palm tree could be another fun alternative for this bag.*

③② Easy T-Shirt Yarn Scarf

This in-between-seasons accessory is a fashion must when it's too hot to wear wool. Forgo a necklace and dress up your wardrobe with this instead.

MATERIALS

2 (13-yard) skeins t-shirt yarn (periwinkle blue)

Scissors

Sewing needle

Coordinating sewing thread

1　Place two ladder-back chairs 36 inches apart. Loop the yarn from both skeins around the backs of the chairs, tying a knot to connect the two skeins when you reach the end of the first one. Leave about 1 arm's length unwrapped from the second skein. Cut this piece off and place it aside.

2　Remove the wrapped yarn from the chairs and tie the beginning and ending loose ends together in a knot.

3　Take the piece of yarn you set aside and wrap it several times around the back of the scarf, covering over the knots.

4　Thread the needle, and sew the wrapped yarn band into place, making sure you tuck in the ends to secure and hide them.

TIP: *A traditional scarf is shown here, but feel free to twist, braid, and add other colors. You could even add beads or old jewelry to dress the scarf up even more.*

Girl's Ric-Rac Removable-Flower Headband

33 (PROJECT)

Young ladies have been decorating their hair with flowers for centuries. This simple-to-make headband can be made with one flower or several to mix and match.

MATERIALS

4 yards sport weight yarn (light blue)

2-inch yarn flower loom plus plastic needle

4 yards sport weight yarn (sage green)

Sewing needle

Thread (sage green)

Silver seed beads

Safety pin

Scissors

Measuring tape

½ yard (1¼-inch) trim (linen)

½ yard (⅜-inch) ric-rac (sage green)

6½-inch strip (⅝-inch) elastic (green)

1   Make a blue flower following the instructions that come with the flower loom. Make it extra-full by wrapping the yarn around the loom at least 3 to 4 times. Use the sage green yarn to make the center, again following the package instructions.

2   Sew 3 seed beads to the center of the flower, then put a safety pin on the back of the flower. Set aside.

3   Cut the linen trim and the ric-rac down to 15 inches long.

4   Hand sew the ric-rac down the center of the linen trim. You could also machine sew or hot glue it if you'd like.

5   Fold the edges of the linen under about ¼ inch on both ends. Place ¼ inch of the end of green elastic on the folded linen (fig. a) and then fold the linen ends in half, sandwiching the elastic between them (fig. b). Hand sew the two sides of the hairband and the elastic together until they are secure. Repeat on the other side of the hairband.

6   Attach the flower about 3 inches in from where the hairband meets the elastic.

TIP: *A child ages 4–9 has a head circumference of about 20½ inches. If you are making this for an older or younger child, you may want to measure the circumference and adjust the pattern accordingly.*

a.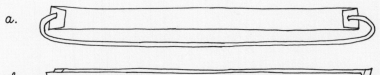

b.

③④ *Yarn and Bead Bib Necklace*

This complex array of coils and rhinestones is deceptively lightweight and very easy to make.

MATERIALS

Newspaper or protective covering for work surface

6 (¾-inch-wide) balsa wood circles

5 (½-inch-wide) balsa wood circles

1 (2-inch-wide) balsa wood circle

Brown paint marker

10 yards each of yarn in two colors (copper and teal)

Scissors

Craft or fabric glue

Disposable bowl

Foam paintbrush

Toothpick

8 x 10-inch piece brown felt

Hot glue gun and glue sticks

Variety pack of circular clear gems

Needle-nose pliers

2 (⅜-inch-wide) ribbon clamps

3 (⅛-inch) jump rings

1 (13-inch-long) chain

Wire cutters

1 lobster clasp

1 (¼-inch) jump ring

1   Place your newspaper down and arrange the wood circles as shown in the photo or to your own taste.

2   Paint all the sides and ⅛ inch around the faces of all your circles with the paint marker and let them dry a few minutes.

3   Cut a piece of copper yarn and a piece of teal yarn each about 12 inches long.

4   Pour some glue into the bowl and, using your foam brush, spread a small amount of glue onto the surface of the largest circle.

5   Leave a 1-inch tail of copper yarn hanging off the edge of the circle. Begin coiling the yarn around the circle, nudging the yarn with both your fingers and a toothpick as needed, making the coils snug against one another. After you have wrapped about half the circle with the copper, switch to the teal yarn and continue the process until the wood circle is covered. Cut the teal yarn close to the wood circle and make sure the end is securely glued down.

6   Dab a little glue on the back of the circle and pull the copper yarn tail to the back. Trim as needed.

7   Repeat Steps 5 to 6 with all of the circles, covering them in either a solid color or two-tone as shown in the photo.

8   Arrange all of the circles onto the felt and position them as shown in the photo or to your own liking, with the largest circle more or less centered.

9   Glue the backs of the wood in place on the felt and let them dry a few minutes.

10   While the glue is drying, heat the hot glue gun with a stick of glue in it.

11   Cut the felt around the design, leaving about a ¾-inch excess of felt around the upper right and upper left circle. This is where you will place your ribbon clamps later.

12   Hot glue your gems into the center of each circle, using the larger gems in the bigger circles and the smaller gems in the smaller circles.

13   Fold the excess felt on the top left in half. Using your needle-nose pliers, place the ribbon clamp over the folded felt and squeeze until the clamp is secure. Repeat this process on the righthand side of the felt.

14   Attach two ⅛-inch jump rings to the ribbon clamps, cut the chain in half with the wire cutters, and attach the chains to the jump rings.

15   Attach the lobster clasp to one of the chains with the remaining ⅛-inch jump ring.

16   Attach the large jump ring to the other chain.

TIP: *If you want the piece to be a little sturdier, use some spray fabric stiffener on the felt before you cut it out.*

(35) Wrap It Up Bracelet

Add a layer of color to your wooden bracelets. Combine one metallic neutral and one brightly colored yarn for perfect harmony on your wrist.

MATERIALS

5 yards sport weight yarn (metallic copper)

5 yards sport weight yarn (teal)

Craft glue

Scissors

Embroidery needle

1. Wrap a wooden bracelet with various colors of yarn, adding small dabs of glue to the inside lip of the bracelet as you go along. Trim the yarn ends as you switch colors and make sure to glue the ends of the yarn to the inside edge of the bracelet as you go along. When you start a new color, wrap over the cut end of the previous color to cover and hold it in place.

2. When you reach the start of your yarn wrapping, cut the yarn, leaving a 2-inch tail. Add a dab of glue under the last wrap. Thread the yarn on the needle and pull the tail underneath the wrapped yarn to hide it.

TIP: *For a really stunning trio of bracelets, make a set of bracelets in copper and teal, copper and blue, and copper and green yarn.*

③⑥ Ombré Tassel Necklace

Make your neckline your best accessory with this beautiful light-to-dark collar.

MATERIALS

10 yards of sport weight ombré yarn (such as Schoppel Wolle Reggae Ombré Yarn)

1 (5 x 3-inch) piece of cardboard

Scissors

1 (13-inch) piece round brown 5 mm leather cord necklace

17 (3/8-inch) wooden beads

Sewing needle

Clear sewing thread

1   Start with the lightest part of the yarn and wrap it around the long side of the cardboard ten times, or until the fibers run the full gamut from light to dark. You may have to experiment with your particular yarn to get the ombré effect, as many yarns vary. Cut the yarn off the cardboard at the bottom.

2   Take three strips of the lightest part of the yarn and fold them in half over the top of the leather cord about 7 inches in from the end of the cord. Make the yarn into a tassel by feeding a bead through the bottom of the yarn and pushing it as close to the top as possible.

3   Repeat Steps 1 and 2, changing the color of the yarn so it goes from light on one end and dark on the other. Make seventeen tassels, or enough to fill the leather necklace so that it resembles a chunky collar. **NOTE:** You can mix a few strands of the color yarn from the previous tassel if you'd like the transition to be smoother. Also, you'll need a bead for every tassel, so plan ahead if you decide to make more.

4   Double thread the sewing needle with the clear thread, and weave the thread in and out of the beads to secure them to the tassels. Tie a knot in the end of the clear thread.

TIP: *To secure the knot in the clear thread, add a little craft glue to the end of it.*

Chapter Three

YARN ART

(37) *Ziggety-Zaggety Key Fob*

The straight pins and yarn wrapped haphazardly on this cross-stitch round are reminiscent of both Mondrian's Broadway Boogie Woogie *and a delectable sugary confection.*

MATERIALS

Small piece of corrugated cardboard, ¼ inch thick

1 (3-inch-round) bamboo cross-stitch round

Black marker

Hot glue gun with glue sticks

Utility knife

Needle-nose pliers

20 multicolored straight pins

Craft glue

Paper plate or bowl

Small scrap of yarn (I used yellow)

Scissors

Fine sewing needle that fits through the needlepoint holes

Dark green felt

Cutting mat

Straight edge ruler

Key chain

1. Place the cardboard on a flat surface. Place the bamboo cross-stitch round on top of the cardboard and trace around the circle with the marker.

2. Heat up the hot glue gun with a stick of glue in it. Cut the circle out of the cardboard with the utility knife and hot glue it to the back of the round.

3. Using wire cutters or needle-nose pliers, cut the metal stems of the straight pins down until they are about ¼ inch long.

4. Place them in the holes around the outer edges of the grid, skipping every other hole.

5. Squeeze a dab of craft glue onto the paper plate and pull the pins out one by one to dip the ends into the glue.

6. Place the pins back into the holes around the outer edges of the grid and let them dry a few minutes.

7. Leaving a tail of about 2 inches, wrap the yarn haphazardly around the pins left to right until it makes a design similar to the one in the photo. Do not cut the yarn.

8. Wrap the same yarn top to bottom until it creates a nice zigzag over the yarn that has already been wrapped. Trim the yarn end, leaving a 2-inch tail.

9. Split the yarn ends of the tail in half and thread the needle with as much yarn as you can get through the eye of the needle. Feed this through one of the holes closest to where you've ended the design. Repeat with the remaining yarn and tie on the back side of the piece. Repeat Step 9 with the other yarn tail.

10. Place the circle, design side facing up, on a small piece of felt and trace around the shape.

11. Cut the felt out and hot glue it to the cardboard on the back of the circle.

12. Place the remaining felt on the cutting mat. Using both the straight edge and the utility knife, cut a 7-inch-long by ¼-inch-wide piece of felt.

13. Hot glue the trim along the outer rim of the circle and cut the excess with scissors.

14. Open the jump ring with the needle-nose pliers, add the fob to the key chain, and close up the jump ring.

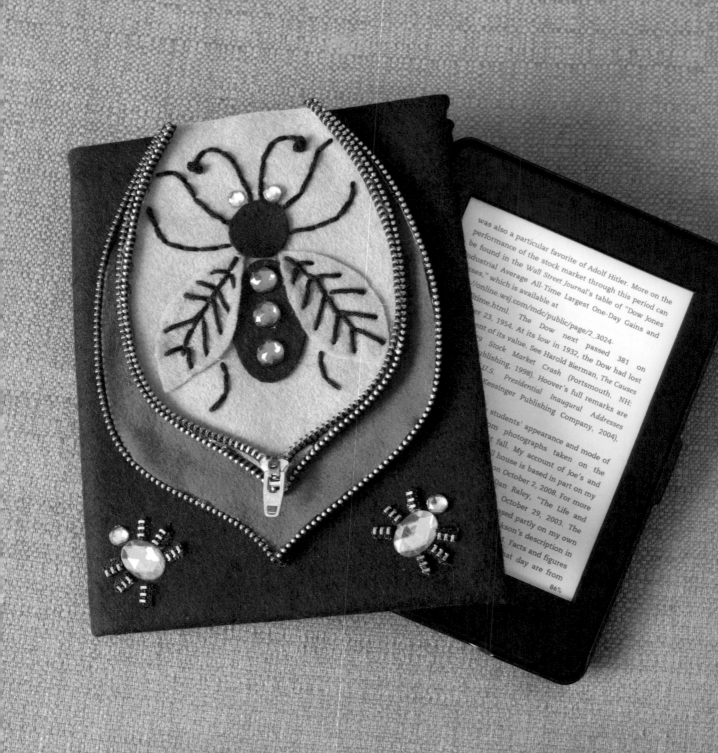

⏺ PROJECT 38 *Zip Your Fly! Kindle Cover*

Turn your cold, black piece of technology into an entomologic work of art.

MATERIALS

Templates from pages 140–143

9 x 12-inch pieces wool felt in five colors (grass green, forest green, sage, mustard, and sky blue)

Scissors

Ruler

Utility knife

1 (8½ x 11-inch) sheet cardboard

Fabric or craft glue

Disposable bowl

Foam paintbrush

Hot glue gun and glue sticks

4 (8-inch) brass zippers with black edging

1 cup hot water

3 yards lightweight cotton yarn (black)

Tapestry needle

2 (¼-inch) rhinestones (pale green)

3 (⅜-inch) rhinestones (turquoise)

2 (⅝ x ¾-inch) long oval rhinestones (amber)

2 (¼-inch) rhinestones (blue)

Adhesive Velcro dots

1   Using the template from page 141, cut out the outer leaf (a) from the grass green felt.

2   Next cut out the inner leaf (b) from the sage green felt.

3   Cut out the head (d) and abdomen (c) and an 8 x 13-inch piece from the forest green felt.

4   Cut out both of the wings (e) from the mustard felt.

5   Cut out a piece of 11½ x 6¾-inch sky blue felt.

6   Cut out two pieces of cardboard the size of your particular e-reader (or use the template on page 142) and center them, side by side, in the middle of the forest green felt. Leave a ½-inch space between the two pieces of cardboard (where a spine would be).

7   Place some of the fabric glue into a disposable bowl and thin it down a bit with a few splashes of hot water. Using the foam paintbrush, glue the cardboard down onto the felt.

8   Using the utility knife, cut 45-degree angles in the felt at the outer corners of the cardboard. Then fold the felt inward and glue it to the cardboard.

9   Lay your green felt-covered cardboard on top of the sky blue felt, and cut the sky blue felt down to the same size. Glue the sky blue felt on top of the exposed cardboard.

10 Set aside while the glue sets up, about 5 minutes. In the meantime, heat up the hot glue gun with a stick of glue in it.

11 Place the grass-green outer leaf (A) on your work surface.

12 Cut an 8-inch length of zipper and trim the fabric down so it's flush with the teeth.

13 Open the zipper, then hot glue the open zipper all around the edge of the leaf, as shown in the picture. **NOTE:** You may want to wet your fingers to avoid getting burned. Cut off any excess after the glue has set.

14 Place the sage green inner leaf (B) on your work surface and repeat Steps 12 to 13.

15 Add a zipper pull directly above the pointy end of the sage green leaf (see photo for placement). Then feed some zipper edges into the zipper pull and glue them into place so it looks like it is an open zipper.

16 Close the cover so the front is facing up. Glue the outer leaf (A) onto the top center of the front cover.

17 Glue the bug head (D) and abdomen (C) into the center of the inner leaf (B).

18 With the black yarn, embroider both the wings (E) as shown in (G), then glue them on top of the bug abdomen (C). Embroider the six legs and the antennae. Make two French knots (see French Knot diagram on page 149) at the ends of each antenna. Glue the inner leaf (B) onto the top center cover on top of the outer leaf (A).

19 Hot glue two pale green rhinestones for the eyes; three turquoise rhinestones in the center of the abdomen; two oval amber rhinestones as shown in the template on the bottom of the cover; and two blue rhinestones to make the eyes on the bottom bugs.

20 Cut twelve 3-tooth lengths of zipper and hot glue them around the amber rhinestones for the legs.

21 Affix a few Velcro dots to the back of your reader, then stick the opposite sides of the Velcro to the inside back of the cover.

(39) *Starry Night Yarn Painting*

This is an updated and modernized yarn craft that I originally found in a 1970s craft magazine. Making a yarn painting is a fun and easy project.

MATERIALS

12 x 12-inch square canvas mounted onto a frame

Pencil

Various scraps of leftover yarn in multiple colors (shades of green, gold, brown, rust, red, and pink)

Fabric glue

Scissors

Toothpick

1   Draw up a pattern on the canvas. I drew 8 circles of varying sizes onto the canvas. Then I worked the yarn around those shapes.

2   If you have thin scraps of yarn, you can braid three strips together for a more substantial result. Or you can start out with bulky yarn and lay the strips down without braiding them.

3   Spread the glue onto the canvas, then cut and adhere the yarn strips onto it. Use a toothpick to help guide the yarn into place. It will take some time to fill up the entire canvas with yarn, but the end result will be beautiful.

TIP: *For a more polished look, place the final artwork into a frame with glass.*

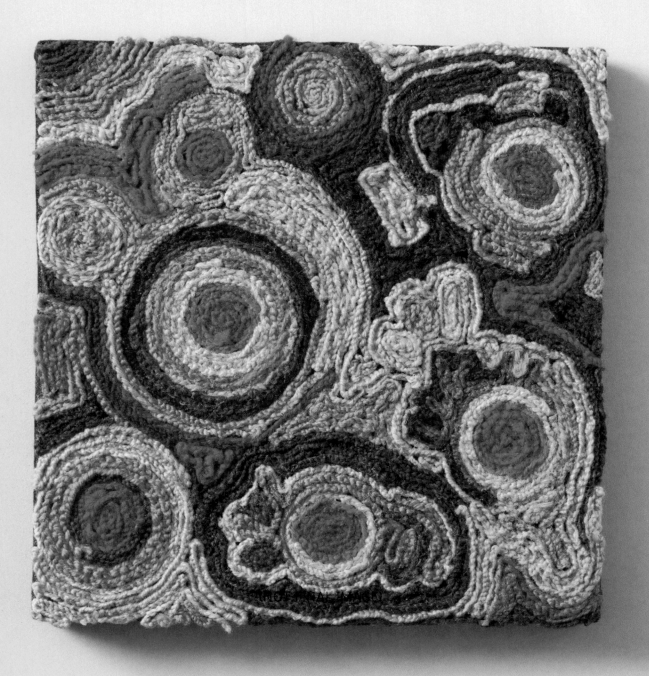

Huichol Indian Yarn Painting

Huichol art is a centuries-old yarn painting technique of the people from the states of Jalisco and Nayarit in Mexico. Its colorful and symbolic style is derived from a ceremonial tablet called the neirika.

MATERIALS

Assorted yarn pieces in multiple colors (scraps or leftover skeins work well)

Pencil

Piece of cardboard or foam board

Craft glue

Toothpick or popsicle stick

1   Take a look at Huichol Indian yarn paintings for inspiration. Traditional yarn paintings have strong contrast, so you may want to consider that when you are selecting your yarn. Here bright yellow and dark blue are used as contrasting colors.

2   Sketch your design onto the cardboard or foam board.

3   Use craft glue to fill one area in at a time. You can spiral your yarn to fill areas or go back and forth in a tight zigzag.

4   Cover the entire board in yarn. Use the toothpick or popsicle stick to push yarn pieces close together.

VARIATION: *You can also experiment with free-form creation. In other words, don't do a sketch, and let your imagination play out as you glue the yarn onto the piece.*

I'm Your Venus String Art

If Botticelli could only see this now! String art gets a new twist and turn as Venus's beautiful tendrils are reconfigured in yarn.

MATERIALS

Template from page 144

Wood or engineered wood board cut down to 26½ x 22½ inches

1 quart white latex paint with eggshell finish

Foam paintbrush

Clear tape

2 (6-ounce) boxes ⅝-inch wire nails

Hammer

20 yards medium weight cotton yarn (dark gray-blue)

Scissors

Craft glue

Disposable plate

Toothpick

2 eyehooks

Picture-hanging wire

1 Photocopy the template from page 144 at 407%. Set it aside.

2 Paint the wood board and let it dry. You may need two coats for full coverage.

3 Tape the template to the center of the board and nail around the lines of the image. Hammer the nail head firmly into the board. When all of the nails have been placed, carefully remove the paper template, keeping as much of it intact as possible to use as a reference.

4 Tie the yarn around the mouth, and start wrapping it around each nail head in a counterclockwise fashion. Look at the template and examine where you placed the nails in it. Follow the yarn all the way around the mouth, connect the yarn to the nose, and start wrapping that.

5 Continue up through the left eyebrow and around the face. Tie off, leaving at least a 2-inch tail. Cut the yarn.

6 There is no particular order in which to wrap the yarn. You have to use your intuition. But a basic rule of thumb is to wrap it as long as you can, then tie it off and start at another section. Wrap the entire outside outline of the hair and the border, then go back and fill in the missing pieces on the inside of the hair, the neck, and the right eye.

7 Once you've wrapped the entire piece, squeeze a small dab of glue onto the plate, and dip your toothpick into the glue. Cut each of the tails that remain hanging and dab the knots with glue. Using your finger, tightly wrap, then glue, any excess yarn to the base of the nail. Hold it in place until the glue starts to set up.

8 Screw two eyehooks into the back of the board and run some picture wire through the eyehooks, then twist it to secure.

> **TIP:** *Print out an extra template at 100% for reference. It will give you a visual to look at while you are deciding how to wrap the yarn around the nails.*

Yarn-Wrapped Air Plant Display

Easy-to-care-for air plants brighten up a window as they hang from this colorfully wrapped stick.

PROJECT 42

MATERIALS

Yarn scraps in a variety of colors (I had about 20 yards total in yellows, browns, and greens)

Stick wide enough to fit across a window

Scissors

Curtain rod brackets or C hooks

Drill

3 small air plant hanging planters

2 medium air plant hanging planters

Bag of small, multicolored rocks

5 air plants

1 Starting about 3 inches in from the end, tie a piece of yarn to the stick, then start wrapping the yarn around it. Wrap the yarn over the knot to cover it. Keep the yarn on the skein until you are done wrapping that individual color, then cut the yarn, leaving a 3-inch tail. Tie the end of the first color together with the second color, and continue wrapping the stick, covering the tails with the yarn you are wrapping. Wrap the yarn various widths for each color to give the piece a random look. Keep switching colors for a striped effect.

2 Once you've wrapped the yarn to about 3 inches from the end of the stick, cut the yarn, leaving about a 6-inch tail. Tie off the yarn, and knot the end. Trim the excess yarn close to the knot.

3 Place your brackets or hooks on the window frame, and place your stick on the brackets.

4 Replace the strings on the planters with different colors of yarn. The replacement strings should measure around 52 inches long. Fold each string in half and place the loop through the center of the glass plant holder (fig. a). Pull the ends of the yarn through the loop (fig. b).

5 Tie the strings onto the stick, overlapping the yarn to make "V" formations as shown in the photo. The plant holders can be hung at varying heights to add interest.

6 Place a small number of rocks in each planter, and add an air plant to each planter.

TIP: *Spinning the stick away from you as you wrap it with yarn makes the process go more smoothly.*

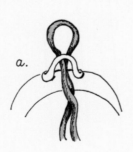

a.

b.

❨43❩ Yarn-Bombed Bicycle

Step aside, graffiti. Yarn-bombing is the latest guerilla warfare to hit the urban landscape. You'll be the hippest bike on the block with this artistic set of wheels.

MATERIALS

Bicycle

5 yards yarn in each of various colors (pink, purple, and turquoise)

Scissors

Yarn needle

Pom-pom maker

1. Wrap the yarn around the frame of the bicycle. Depending on the shape, size, and intended pattern, you'll wrap as needed, changing colors, to fully cover the frame. As you change colors, tie a knot between the old and new yarn, leaving a 3-inch tail each time. When you are finished with the bike, thread the yarn needle, and weave the tails back into the wrapped portion.

2. Continue wrapping the handlebars, crank arm for the pedals, and seat post in the same manner as Step 1.

3. Weave pink, purple, and turquoise yarn around the front spokes as shown.

4. For the back spokes, wrap each spoke individually, tying a knot at the end of each spoke.

5. Follow directions on the pom-pom maker and attach them to the ends of your handlebars.

FUN IDEA: *Yarn-bomb your bike lock or basket to match.*

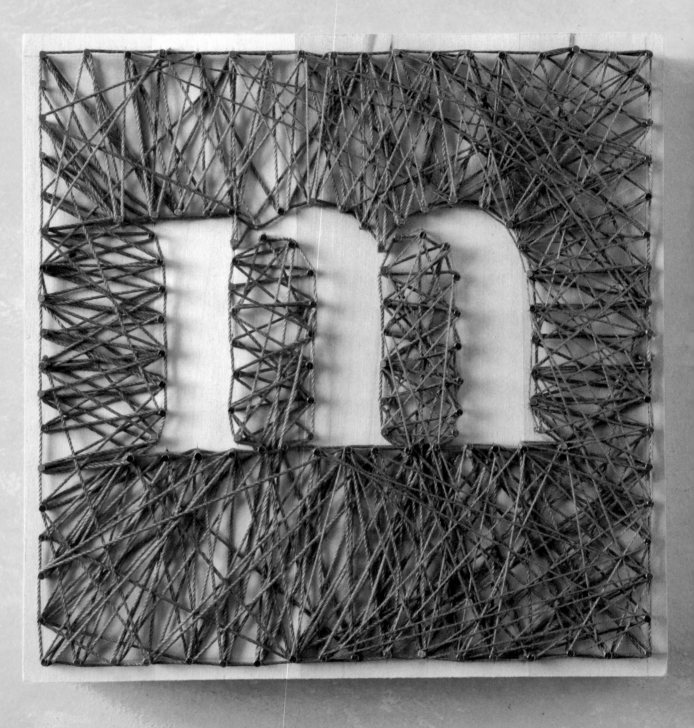

⊙44 *String Art Initial*

Need artwork for your walls but don't want to spend a lot of cash? Personalize your walls with this beautiful ombré-colored letterform.

MATERIALS

Scissors

Lowercase initial printed onto a sheet of paper with a 7½-inch square border

Clear tape

1 (8 x 8-inch) piece of wood

½-inch wire nails

Hammer

1 skein (184 yards) each of light-weight cotton tatting yarn in three colors (blue, teal, and olive)

1   Cut out your initial printout around the border, then tape it onto the piece of wood.

2   Hammer your nails around the initial and the border, about ½ inch apart. You can use a ruler or measuring tape if you want them to be perfectly spaced. Otherwise you can just eyeball it.

3   Take the blue yarn (leaving it on the skein or ball) and wrap it around the letterform, outlining the shape. The best way is to wrap the yarn counterclockwise around each nail head, pulling it tight and continuing on to the nail head next to it.

4   Once the initial has been outlined, work your way out to the bottom outside nails on the border. This can be done randomly, wrapping around an outside nail and then back to one of the nails that make up the initial, until you get the look you want and the bottom of the piece has the desired density. Cut the yarn, leaving a 2-inch tail, knot the yarn at one of the nail heads, then bury the tail under the woven parts of the piece.

5   Continue with the blue yarn in the upper lefthand corner, working randomly back and forth counterclockwise until you are halfway around the square. Tie off the blue yarn.

6   Tie on the teal yarn and overlap the blue in the lower lefthand corner. Continue wrapping randomly until the rest of the square has been wrapped. Make sure you fill in the spaces between the letterforms and outline the edges of the initial with yarn as you go along to give the piece strongly defined edges.

7   Tie the olive yarn onto the bottom righthand side of the piece, and wrap another layer over the teal. This layer should be wrapped here and there, not too densely. The desired effect is to add an extra layer of color to give it some dimension and an ombré effect.

TIP: *Screw some c-hooks into the base and make a personalized necklace holder or a key holder.*

Floating Photo

Instead of putting your photo in a traditional mat, consider sewing it into the frame. This is a surprising way to make your image look as if it is suspended in the air.

MATERIALS

1 (19½-inch) square white frame with picture mat and removable inner frame

Flat-head screwdriver

1 (20 x 30-inch) sheet white watercolor paper

Self-healing cutting mat

Pencil

Metal ruler

Utility knife

12-inch square dry-mounted photo

1 sheet standard-ruled notebook paper

Tapestry needle

White eraser

Drill

⅛-inch drill bit

Heavy-duty tape

1 skein (184 yards) lightweight yarn (yellow)

Scissors

1   Flip the frame over and use the screwdriver to take the backing off the frame.

2   Place the watercolor paper on your self-healing mat, then place the picture mat over the watercolor paper. Trace around the outside of the picture mat with the pencil and then cut out the shape with the ruler and the utility knife. **NOTE:** Do not trace or cut out the inside opening of the picture mat. Place aside.

3   Place your photo face up on your work surface. Draw a square pencil line all the way around the photo ¼ inch in from the edge of the photo. Place a sheet of the lined notebook paper on the edges of the pencil lines and mark off every other line for a total of seventeen tick marks on both the top and bottom of the square. Then mark off fifteen holes on both the left and right of the frame, again marking every other line. The total number of tick marks should be sixty-four.

4 Puncture each of the marks with the tapestry needle, then erase any remaining pencil marks. Place aside.

5 Draw a pencil line to mark the middle of the inside of the inner picture frame on all four sides. Measure out (then mark with a pencil) eighteen evenly spaced holes on each side of the inside of the picture frame, approximately 1 inch apart. Drill holes in the areas marked.

6 Place the inner frame on your work surface. Tape it down at the corners, making sure you don't cover the drilled holes with the tape. Make a tape roll and adhere it to the back of the photo. Center the photo in the middle of your inner frame, tamping it down so the photo sticks to your work surface.

7 Measure 5 arm's lengths worth of yarn. Single thread the needle with the yarn, and make several knots in the end of the yarn.

8 Pull the yarn through the back of the photo until it stops at the knot. Then start sewing the yarn from the front of the photo to one of the holes in the edge of the frame. Then bring the yarn back through another hole on the outside of the frame, in through the hole and back over the photo. This is done in a very random fashion. It should zigzag from picture hole to frame hole until all of the holes are filled.

9 Bring the yarn up over the picture hole one last time and tie a knot in the end on the underside of the picture. **NOTE:** You will probably run out of yarn while you are doing this process so just repeat Step 8 as many times as you need.

10 Clean the glass, place the inner frame within the outer frame, place the watercolor paper behind that and place the backing and hardware onto the frame.

VARIATION: *Use a black and white photo and some red yarn or baker's string.*

PROJECT 46 Oh Deer! Holiday Card Holder

Have you ever tried to figure out a fun way to organize your holiday cards? This deer head will keep them neatly displayed for years to come.

MATERIALS

1 (17 x 1-inch) unfinished wood round

Drop cloth or newspapers

Matte black spray paint and primer in one

Template from page 138

Scissors

Clear tape

18 ($5/8$-inch) wire nails

Hammer

Tweezers or utility knife

1 (184-yard) skein tatting yarn (off-white)

Craft glue

1 (184-yard) skein tatting yarn (red)

1 quart water-based paint stain (red)

Disposable bowl

44 ($13/4$-inch) mini wood spring clothespins

Foam paintbrush

Wooden skewers

Hot glue gun and glue sticks

Utility knife

1. Place the wooden round on a drop cloth or newspapers.

2. Spray paint the front and sides of the round with the black paint. Paint in a well-ventilated area. Outside is ideal, but if the weather is not good, make sure to open the windows and use a fan. Apply two coats of paint and follow manufacturer's directions for drying times.

3. Make a copy of the template from page 138 at 225% size. Cut out the circle.

4. Tape the template to the wood round, making sure it is centered on the round.

5. Starting with the deer head, hammer the nails around the shape of the deer, spacing each nail about ¼ inch apart.

6. Do the same with the circle, using the grid lines to help line up and place your nails.

7. Once all of the nails are in place, remove the template by tearing it off the board. There may be a few paper scraps that you can remove with a pair of tweezers or a utility knife.

8. Leaving the off-white yarn on the skein or ball, tie the yarn end in a knot onto one of the nails. Begin by looping the yarn around each nail head around the outside of the deer to define the shape.

9. To fill in the shape of the deer head, wrap the yarn randomly around the nail heads, crisscrossing and overlapping until the deer head is defined and stands out against the black background. Tie a knot in the yarn and trim the end. You can either bury the tail, or cut it close to the nail head and add a drop of glue to the knot to secure it.

10. Leaving the red yarn on the skein or ball, begin by tying the yarn end in a knot onto one of the nails in the outside circle. Begin by looping the yarn around each nail head around the outside of the circle to define it. Tie the ends in a knot and place a small dab of glue on the knot. Cut the ends as close as you can to the knot.

11 Place some stain into the bowl.

12 Drop the clothespins into the bowl and let them soak for about 10 minutes.

13 Wash the excess stain off the clothespins and touch them up with the foam paintbrush where more saturation of color is needed.

14 Clip the clothespins onto the skewer and set the skewer over the bowl. Let the paint stain dry according to the directions on the container.

15 Turn on the hot glue gun with a stick of glue in it. Place the clothespins with the clip facing out between every other nail around the outside perimeter. Hot glue the clothespins in place, making sure the bottom of each clothespin fits under the yarn.

TIP: *Print out a second copy of the deer head template. This will be a great reference as you do the outline of the deer head.*

TIP: *Buy pre-stained red clothespins to eliminate Steps 11 through 14.*

Chapter Four

CARDS AND GIFTS

Personalized Initial Notebook

PROJECT 47

Embroider a felt notebook with a soft, dimensional letter.

MATERIALS

Dark gray felt notebook

White transfer paper

Pencil

5 yards each of lightweight yarn in two colors (pink and yellow)

Tapestry needle

Scissors

1. Choose an alphabet letter you like and transfer it onto the notebook following the transfer paper package instructions. **NOTE:** You may have to go over the design several times to make the transfer work.

2. Single thread the needle with the yellow yarn and tie a knot at the end. Embroider around the outside edge of the letter using the backstitch technique shown on page 149. Then fill in the inside of the letter. When finished, pull the yarn through to the backside of the project and tie a knot at the end of the yarn. Trim the excess yarn at the end of the knot.

3. Single thread the needle with the pink yarn, tie a knot at the end, and backstitch the lines of the shadow of the letter. When finished, pull the yarn through to the backside of the project and tie a knot at the end of the yarn. Trim the excess yarn at the end of the knot.

VARIATION: *Need a guestbook? Try a script letter for a fancier, more traditional look.*

Multicolored Embroidered Notecards

The same combination of yarns, used in three different patterns, makes up this eye-catching series.

MATERIALS

**Template of your choice
from pages 146–148**

Scissors

Number 2 pencil

4 x 6-inch blank white notecards

White drafting tape

5 yards yarn in each of 4 colors

Embroidery needle

White eraser

1   Photocopy one of the templates from pages 146–148 and cut it out.

2   Using the side of the tip of the number 2 pencil, turn the photocopied template over, design side facing down, and rub the pencil over the back of the page.

3   Flip the photocopy over, design side facing up, and place the front of the notecard under it.

4   Tape the card and the photocopy down, and trace firmly over the front of the design until the image is transferred onto the card.

5   Embroider the image onto the card using the backstitch technique shown on page 149.

6   Tie off the ends as you finish each color.

7   Use the white eraser to erase any pencil lines that are showing after you finish embroidering the card.

> **TIP:** *Another technique is to poke little holes around the design with the needle before you start embroidering. Then erase the pencil marks. This makes cleaning up eraser debris much easier, since it won't get stuck on the embroidery.*

⟨49⟩ On the Wire Greeting Cards

Use a single strand of leftover yarn to make a high wire, and both an outside and inside telephone wire.

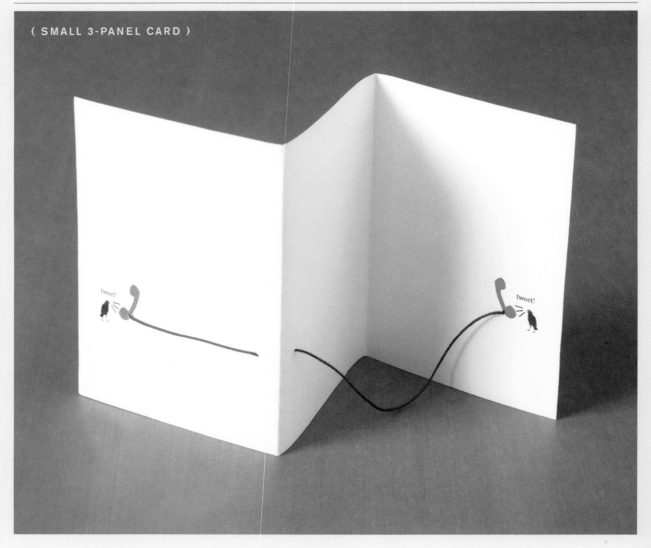

(SMALL 3-PANEL CARD)

tweet!

tweet!

(LARGE CARDS)

MATERIALS

Stock photography

1 (8½ x 11-inch) sheet
card stock (you'll need 2
sheets if making both kinds)

Cutting mat

Utility knife

White glue

Disposable plate

2 feet red yarn

Scissors

Toothpick

Straight edge ruler

Tapestry needle (for the small
card only)

For the larger card
(FITS IN A 4¾ X 6½-INCH ENVELOPE, A6):

1 Purchase then download artwork from a
   stock photo agency of your choice (I used
   istockphoto.com).

2 Using a software layout program of
   your choice, create a card 6¼ inches x
   9 inches. The actual live area for your
   image will be 6¼ inches x 4½ inches and
   will take up the bottom half of the card.

127

3   Place your image on the card and typeset whichever words you would like the greeting to say.

4   Print onto an 8½ x 11-inch sheet of card stock. Cut and fold the card in half vertically. The folded card will measure 6¼ x 4½ inches.

5   Place a small amount of glue on the plate and dip the toothpick into the glue. Place a small amount of glue onto the piece of red yarn. Glue the yarn on the horizon line of the card.

For the small, 3-panel card
(FITS IN A 4-BAR, OR 3⅝ X 5⅛-INCH ENVELOPE):

1   Purchase then download artwork from a stock photo agency of your choice (I used istockphoto.com).

2   Using a software layout program of your choice, create a card 10½ x 4⅞ inches. Divide the card into three sections. The live area for your image on each panel will be 3½ x 4½ inches.

3   Place your images on the card and typeset whichever words you would like the greeting to say.

4   Print onto an 8½ x 11-inch sheet of card stock. Cut and fold the card into the three sections accordion-style (also known as a z-fold). The folded card will measure 3½ x 4½ inches.

5   Single thread the tapestry needle with a 12-inch length of red yarn and knot the end of the yarn. Pierce through the folded card with the needle about ½ inch from the righthand edge of the front fold. Sew through the hole in the back of the card and up through the holes in the second fold. Lay the card flat and stretch the yarn across the flattened card. Sew the yarn to the card on the third (lefthand) panel and tie a knot in the back. Trim ends with scissors.

OTHER IDEAS: *Find art showing a person on a tight rope, two people playing tug of war, two cans joined by a string, or a person walking a dog on a leash.*

PROJECT 50 No Mo' Bows Gift Wrap

Let the most elegant package on the gift table be a hallmark of your good taste and creativity.

MATERIALS

Solid color wrapping paper (matte wrapping paper used here)

Scissors

Masking tape

Template from page 145

Number 2 pencil

5½-inch round card

Tapestry needle

Medium weight yarn (amount needed based on size of present)

1 sheet of Japanese or decorative wrapping paper

Stapler

Heavy-duty adhesive-backed Velcro

½-inch round adhesive-backed gem

1. Wrap the present.

2. Photocopy the template from page 145 and rub the back of the template with pencil.

3. Place a 5½-inch round card on your work surface and tape down. Flip the template over (right-side-up), place on top of the card, and trace over the holes on the template with a pencil, transferring the design onto the round card.

4. Using a tapestry needle, poke holes through the card in the areas you just transferred onto the card.

5. Cut 12 lengths of yarn that are at least the circumference of your package plus 6 inches.

6. Thread the tapestry needle with a single strand of the yarn. Sew the yarn through the holes: in through the front hole and out the back, then bring the needle up through the back of the hole directly across from it. Leave an equal amount of yarn ends on the outside of your card (see fig. a). You will use this to tie the card to the present.

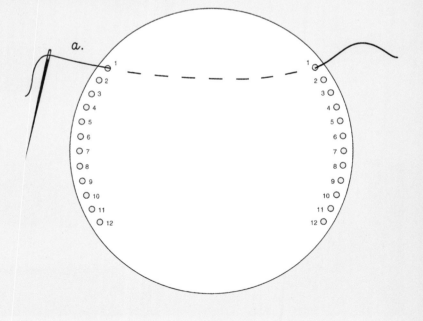

7 Follow Step 6, going through the second set of holes.

8 Repeat Step 6 until all twelve holes have been threaded with the yarn.

9 Lightly tape the card to the center of the wrapped box, so that the paper doesn't tear.

10 Pull all the strands from one side of the card around to the back of the wrapped gift and temporarily tape them to the back of the box. Make sure to keep the loose strands from crossing over one another. They should be evenly spaced like the strings of a guitar, and not overlap.

11 Repeat Step 10 on the remaining side, gathering the yarn around to the back of the wrapped gift.

12 Take off the tape on the back and tie all of the strands together in a knot.

13 Trim the ends.

14 For the decorative, accordion-folded circle: Cut out a 4½ x 11-inch sheet of the decorative paper.

15 Turn the sheet so the 4½-inch side of the paper is closest to you. Starting at the bottom of the sheet, fold the sheet accordion-style. Each segment should be about ½ inch wide (fig. b). The completely folded sheet should measure 4½ x ½ inch.

16 Fold the sheet in half, as shown in fig. c. Staple it in the middle (see fig. d).

17 Open out the fan on top and bottom and staple left and right sides together to close up the top of the fan circle (see fig. e).

b.

c.

d.

e.

18 Repeat Step 17 on the bottom of the fan as well.

19 Velcro the fanned-out circle onto the 5½-inch round card.

20 Adhere a gem to the center of the fanned-out circle.

TIP: *Try adding a strip of the decorative paper to the center of the package and braiding the yarn (bottom package in photo).*

ANOTHER IDEA: *Make the packaging without the 5½-inch card and simply wrap the yarn three times around the package (center package in photo).*

Templates

SPUTNIK LAMPSHADE (ENLARGE TO 120%)

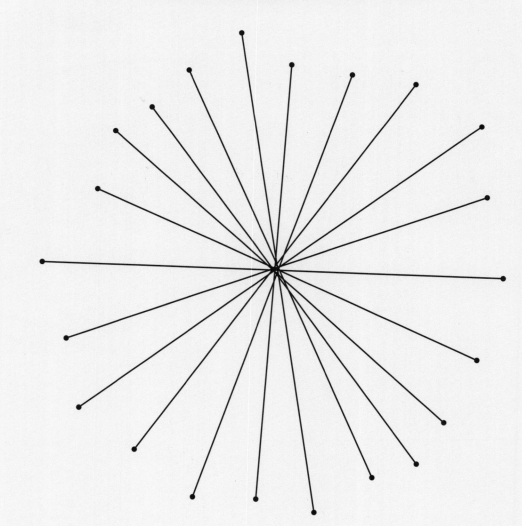

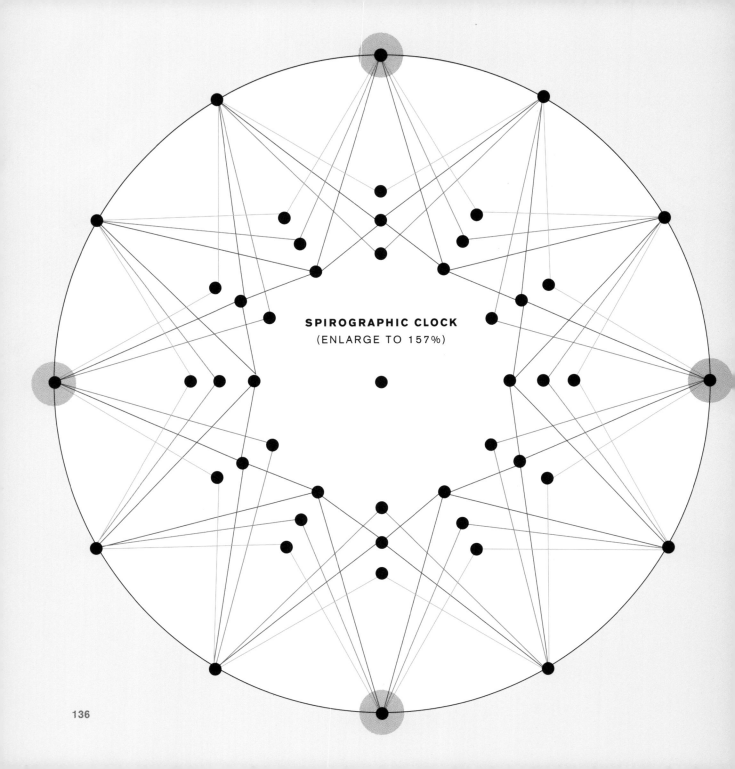

SPIROGRAPHIC CLOCK

(ENLARGE TO 157%)

TISSUE BOX PATTERN (SHOWN AT 100%)

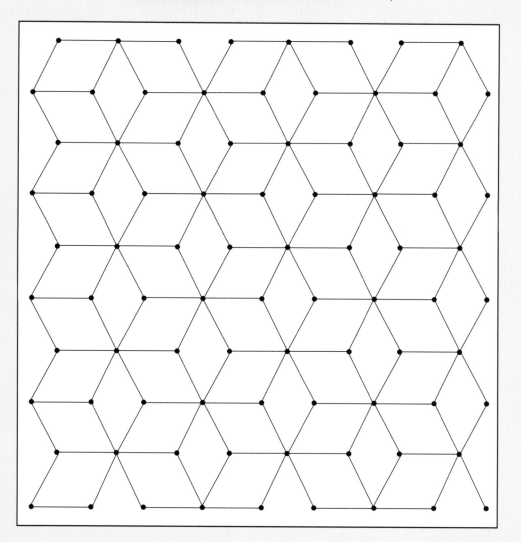

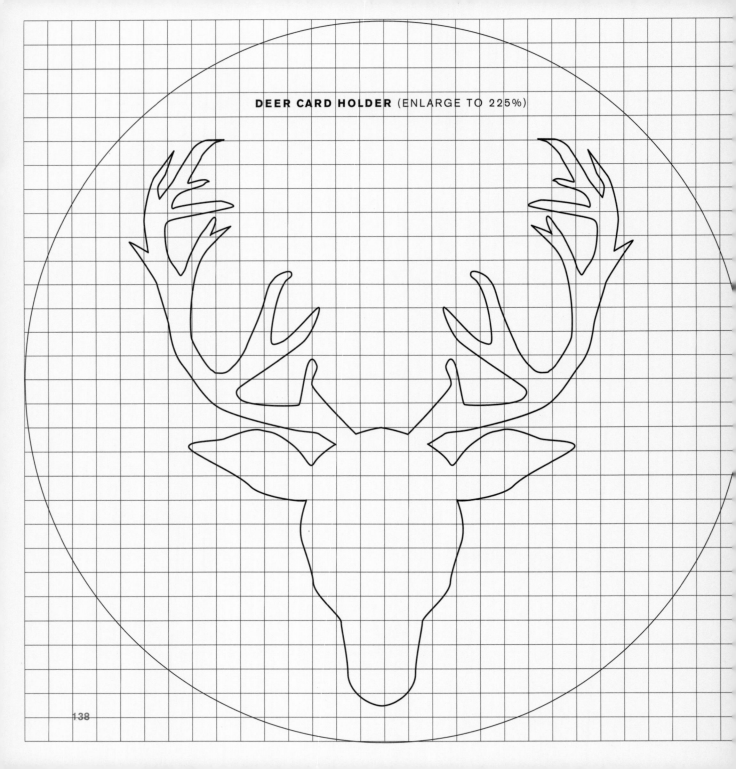

DEER CARD HOLDER (ENLARGE TO 225%)

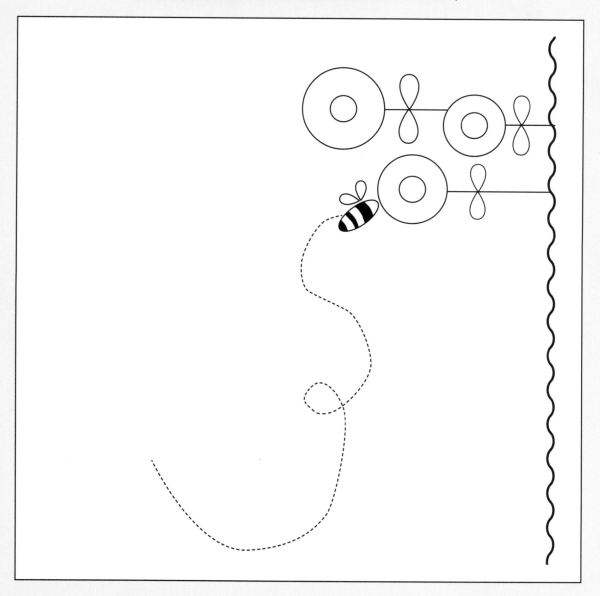

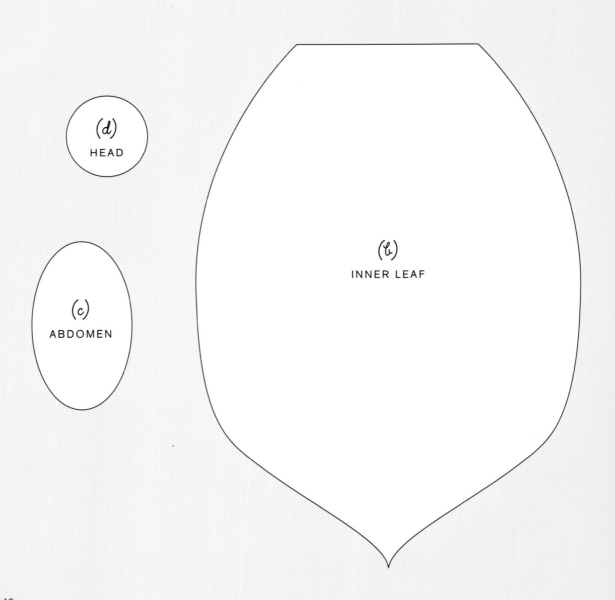

(d)
HEAD

(c)
ABDOMEN

(b)
INNER LEAF

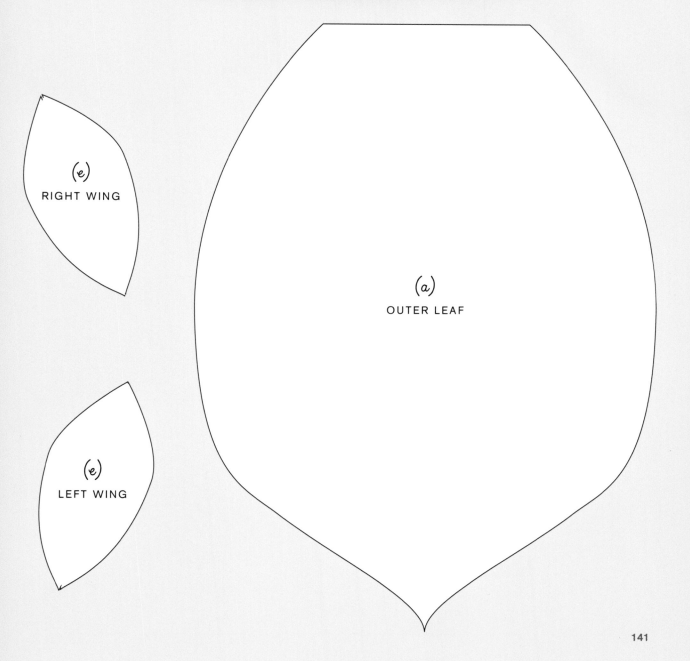

(f.)

BOOK BOARD

Cut out 2

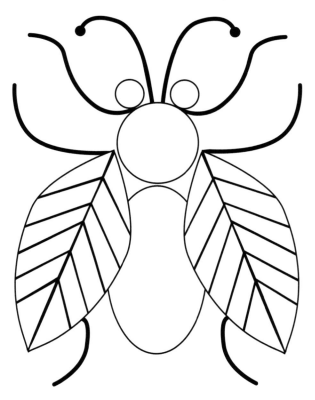

(g.)

PLACEMENT TEMPLATE

VENUS STRING ART (ENLARGE TO 407%)

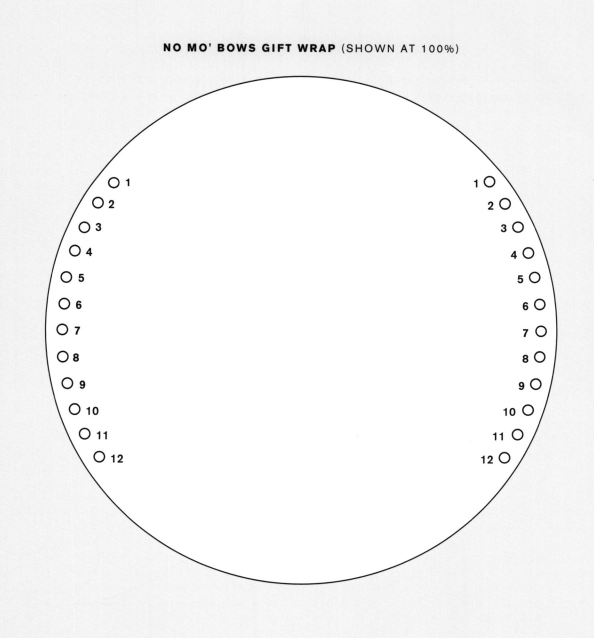

MULTICOLORED EMBROIDERED NOTECARDS "AMOEBA" (SHOWN AT 100%)

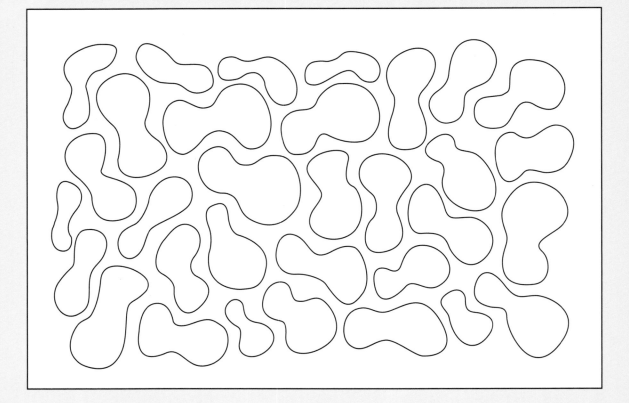

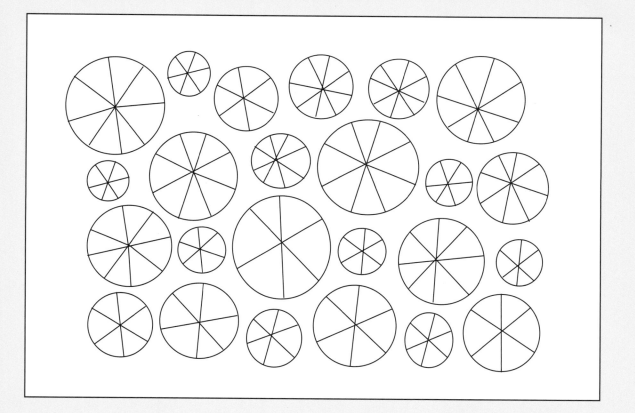

MULTICOLORED EMBROIDERED NOTECARDS "BALUSTRADE" (SHOWN AT 100%)

Backstitch

French Knot

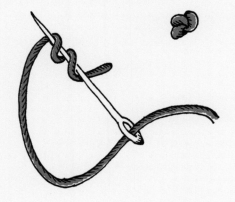

Contributors

An outpouring of love and thanks to all of the contributors who helped me make projects, brainstormed with me, and created ideas of their own. I am forever grateful for all of you, and there is no way I could have done it without you.

PROJECT 2. **Pom-Pom Chair: Alex and Lina Zink, pom-pom makers**

PROJECTS 3 AND 46. **Picture Perfect Earring Frame and String Art Initials by Margot Grisar**

PROJECT 5. **Upcycled Lawn Chair: designer, Andrea Renzi McFadden; concept, Jeanmarie Fiocchi Marden**

PROJECTS 6 AND 21. **String Art Lampshade and From Here to Infinity Braided Scarf with Pom-Poms by Carolynn DeCillo**

PROJECT 13. **Mom Loves "U" Yarn-Hooked Pillow by Lilla Rogers**

PROJECTS 22 AND 37. **Pom-Pom Covered Slippers and Wrap It Up Bracelet by Ingrid Schorr**

PROJECT 32. **Easy T-Shirt Yarn Scarf by Malika Oyetimein/LoveLolaKnits**

PROJECT 39. **Starry Night Yarn Painting by Madeleine Zetterberg**

PROJECT 40. **Huichol Indian Yarn Painting by Katie Lipsitt**

PROJECT 43. **Yarn-Bombed Bicycle by Rebecca Snotflower**

PROJECT 45: **Floating Photo photograph by Peter Dixon**

Acknowledgments

There are so many people involved in bringing a book from an idea into a printed piece.

Here are some of the folks I am aware of, and I thank anyone involved behind the scenes whom I don't know.

First, I'd like to thank my agents, Holly Schmidt and Allan Penn at Hollan Publishing, for coming up with the book concept and finding a publisher. I'd also like to thank Allan for photographing all of the projects.

Second, I would like to give thanks to Kristen Green Wiewora, our editor, and Susan Van Horn, our art director, and all of the folks at Running Press for making beautiful sense out of all of this work.

Additionally, I'd like to thank my beautiful models and their parents for allowing them to be photographed: Isabela Salas-Betsch, Silvia Dowdell, and my niece, Eliza Roessler. Also, big hugs to my incredibly generous friends Laura Bayne and Carolynn DeCillo for photographing the projects for the prototype. And last, but not least, my sister Bridget, who paid half the bus fare for Eliza.

Index

Page numbers in *italics* indicate photographs.

Notes:

Notes: